KT-550-107

Children Making Music

Accession no.
00987955

TRICIA BINNS

WITHDRAWN

LIBRARY

TEL. 01244 375444 EXT. 3301

This book is to be returned on or
before the last date stamped below.
Overdue charges will be incurred by
the late return of books.

UNIVERSITY
COLLEGE
CHESTER

A College of the
University of Liverpool

3/4 9.30a

CANCELLED

28/05/04 .
9.30am (AH)

20/05/04
12: 24pm

WITHDRAWN

Short Loan

THIS BOOK **MUST** BE ISSUED AT
THE COUNTER IF YOU WISH TO USE IT
OUTSIDE THE SHORT LOAN AREA

Children Making Music

Tricia Binns

. 1179937

LIBRARY
ACC. No. 00987955 DEPT. SL
CLASS No. 372.87044 BIN
UNIVERSITY
COLLEGE CHESTER

SIMON & SCHUSTER
EDUCATION

© Tricia Binns 1994

First published in 1994 by
Simon & Schuster Education
Campus 400, Maylands Avenue,
Hemel Hempstead, Herts HP2 7EZ
United Kingdom

All rights reserved. No part of this publication may be
reproduced, stored in a retrieval system, or transmitted in any
form or by any means, electronic, mechanical, photocopying or
otherwise, without the prior permission of the publisher.

British Library Cataloguing in Publication Data is
available from the British Library

ISBN 0 7501 0458 9

Typeset by MHL Typesetting Ltd, Coventry
Printed by Redwood Books, Trowbridge

Contents

Acknowledgements   viii

Introduction   1

1   Using the voice   5

2   Work with percussion   20

3   Music and language   39

4   Scoring   56

5   Science and sound   72

6   Cross-curricular music   81

7   Assessment and recording   91

8   General musical activities and resources   103

Conclusion   115

Acknowledgements

I would like to thank Mrs K M Chacksfield, Headmistress (until 1981) of Chandlers Ford County Infant School, Hampshire for giving me the inspiration and opportunity to develop the teaching methods described in this book and also the staff of the school at that time. Thanks are due also to Mr R Fletcher, Senior Music Advisor to Hampshire Education Department, for his encouragement.

I would also like to thank Mr M Lormor, Senior Music Advisor to Sefton Education Department for his help especially in the chapter on assessment and recording. My thanks go too to the staff and children of the following primary schools:

   Atherton House School, Blundellsands, Liverpool
   Crosby Road North School, Crosby, Liverpool
   St Raymonds School, Harrop Croft, Liverpool
   Kew Woods School, Southport
   Marshside School, Southport
   Freshfield School, Freshfield
   Litherland Moss School, Litherland, Liverpool
   Our Lady of Lourdes School, Southport

Thanks are also due to the Headmaster and staff of Summerhill School, Maghull, Liverpool, especially the music specialist, Mrs Brenda Pomfret, for allowing Mr Alan Edwards to take photographs, and to Mrs Alison Grace and children in year 6 for the carol. Thanks are also due to Mrs Glenys Trafford for secretarial assistance, to Mr Henry Pluckrose and Prof. Leonie Burton for their advice and assistance and to the Education Department, The Royal Opera House, London WC2 for permission to use photographs by Mr Donald Southern and Ms Leila Miller.

Finally I would like to express my thanks to my daughters Louise and Jane for their unfailing support, and also to all the children I have taught.

                                                              Tricia Binns

Introduction

This book is written to help the non-specialist music teacher faced with the implementation of the National Curriculum, who feels unable to teach anything but the simplest songs and sometimes not even those. It is designed to show that music need not be something that happens for an hour on a Tuesday morning or on a Friday afternoon, or when the peripatetic instrumental teacher is in school to take the fortunate few. Hopefully the following chapters will give ideas on where to begin, how to progress and demonstrate that once begun, music can become a living and important part of life and work in the classroom.

Eighteen years ago in a primary school in Hampshire the headteacher gave me the opportunity to give up my other subjects and take music throughout the school. Even with a musical background, a fully trained singing voice and having taken music as a main subject at college I found the prospect daunting. I had always sung with children but this was going to be something different. Because of falling roles there was a spare classroom, there was also a limited amount of money. The school possessed several rusty triangles and cymbals and that was all. The headmistress and I began to make the room as attractive as possible with carpet, curtains, new chairs and occasional tables on which to display our starting pack of small percussion instruments. We also purchased music charts, records, tapes and some books about music. I decided against using one particular scheme but after some research took what I thought we might need from the schemes available at the time. In the school there was a record player, a tape recorder and pianos, the oldest of which we placed in the room, mainly for the children to use as I was not a pianist at that time. The room was very attractive and the children saw their time there as a great treat. From the beginning we stressed care of the instruments and other resources and although we had everything permanently on display there was very little damage.

At first I worked in isolation. Apart from hymn practice in the hall one morning a week, my time was carefully divided between the classes so that each child in the school came to the music room at least once a week, either in a group or with the whole class, depending upon the wish of the class teacher. I did insist that every child came, not just the disruptive ones, to enable the teacher to get on with some 'real work', or, at the other end of the scale, all the class except those who needed some extra help with reading or maths. I felt that we were at the start of something worthwhile and each child should participate equally. My plan was to teach music as I had been trained to teach every other primary school subject, so using these methods I made flashcards for the names of the instruments, put lists of relevant words up around the room and began to devise the activities described in the following chapters. Children's work of any standard in this field was very important and I displayed it all on the walls and in large class books. I made a point of showing the class teacher what we had been doing and either giving her/him some of the written work and art to display or inviting her/him in to listen to our music making. Eventually the children began to relate what was happening in their classrooms to what we were doing together and a link began.

Another breakthrough came when the headteacher asked each class teacher in turn to organise one class assembly each week to which parents would be invited. I offered to help with the music and the teacher became involved with the choice of suitable hymns and which piece of music to play as the children came into the hall to provide the right atmosphere for what was to follow. This became the norm and after a time the assembly became a vehicle for singing or performing our compositions. We accompanied hymns with percussion, showed any artwork related to music, used percussion to enhance the dramatised bible stories, even dancing to the 'Hava N'Guila' during the story of the Marriage Feast at Cana.

Gradually the class teachers became more involved in what was happening and we began to team teach. The staff set up sound corners in their classrooms and were very keen to display any children's work in the classroom. In time the music making could happen in the music room, classroom, hall or all three places depending on what was needed. The timetable became more flexible especially in the afternoons and we set one afternoon aside as a music workshop and any child or group of children could move freely from their classes into the music room to work. By this time the children were used to the concept of music making being an ongoing situation with freely available instruments and sound-producing objects and they used these extra resources in the same way that they used art materials to enhance and give another dimension to their general work.

This ad hoc discovery took place in a carefully planned environment and scheme of work. Good teachers, even those who think of themselves as non-musical can see possibilities of which the child is often only half aware. This is the skill of knowing when and how to intervene. The children were very enthusiastic and surprising us all the time with the level of work they were producing, and none of this enthusiasm had to be dampened. As music specialist I taught the more formal aspects of music whenever I saw the opportunity, again keeping the enthusiasm alive and not becoming a bore.

Sometimes the children themselves asked for the more formal aspects to be put into their work. One of the most exciting developments was the children's own method of scoring as described in later chapters. We were one of the first schools to work in this way and the non-specialist teacher did not need any expertise in scoring to understand and encourage this way of working.

A peripatetic violin teacher was appointed and found the atmosphere in the school very conducive to her work. Parents attended the violin lessons and some brought their own violins, whilst others were lent a violin by the county so that they could participate. Some parents took piano lessons so that they could accompany the violin and recorder practice at home. We took children to hear local concerts so that they could experience live music making and found them very responsive. We liaised with our comprehensive school. Groups of GCSE students came to work with the children and we took advantage of their well equipped drama room and large percussion instruments on return visits.

Any parent with musical ability came in to perform. We had a classical pianist as well as a jazz trumpeter who spent some time learning to play nursery rhymes only to find that we preferred jazz! One parent who was a potter made us a series of pipes. Children joined local junior orchestras and later area orchestras. Some are now playing in the large orchestras as professional musicians. Hopefully several more have acquired a love of music and are pursuing it as a leisure interest.

These kind of results take time to achieve, but with encouragement teachers can build upon their own strengths and skills. Some of the activities described in the book may not be seen as being music based but more as language, science or maths involving music. Many of the ideas in the book come from the children who, given the environment and opportunity, gain confidence in their own creative powers in music and will take the sensitive teacher along with them. No educational scheme can work alone, the quality of the teaching is paramount and the ideas will only be successful if the teacher has confidence enough to have a go. With the National Curriculum now requiring every pupil to be taught music, this book will hopefully give some starting points for the non-specialist to try. Music making provides children with an opportunity to achieve something positive. They can experience the satisfaction of producing an original composition, of giving a good performance and of discovering a new piece of music to enjoy.

1 Using the voice

The voice is the child's first means of musical expression. Baby's voice varies greatly in pitch and is strong and loud, or quiet and murmuring, and a parent learns very quickly what each sound means — hunger, discomfort, anger or just plain boredom. The voice plays an important part therefore in developing the child's musicality. Each child's voice is unique and is an individual means of expression and communication. Babies develop their own singing language and croon away to themselves. Toddlers will sing over and over again a phrase or tune which catches their fancy. They can be heard in shops, in the home, and when older, in school or in the playground.

Michael, a 6-year-old boy from Hong Kong whose English is not yet very fluent, sings away to himself all day in his classroom. We encouraged Michael to sing and commented favourably on his ability to hold a tune. He gained enough in confidence to sing a number song in Chinese to the class. His older cousin translated it and we taught the English translation to the class. Michael sang in Chinese and we followed in English. His status in the class increased as the children realised that Michael could speak two languages.

Michael's song

All too often, children come to school and are immediately inhibited when their creative vocal activities are stopped in the name of discipline. There may be a formal singing lesson once a week with the teacher who can play the piano. The teacher often sits with her/his back to the children, or at least, side on. The children are expected to learn the words and the rhythm whether they understand the words or not, as well as sitting up straight and singing up. Young children can use their vocal powers to make sounds of varying pitch, length, speed, volume and true colour.

Singing with children

There are heavy demands placed upon the non-specialist teacher with limited vocal skills but most teachers find that the more they sing the better they become and the more confidence they acquire. They then begin to enjoy singing, and this enjoyment is transmitted to the children they teach. Children do not expect a professional sound and they are so keen to join in and show what they can do that they are not critical of the teacher as long as the words and tune are there for them to learn. It is not necessary to be a pianist to teach singing. You can learn songs from a tape or persuade a colleague who can play the piano to teach or tape a tune for you. Children learn more quickly from a live performance and young children enjoy sitting in front of the teacher watching her/his face and lips. Tapes are often too fast and too high and are therefore a last resort.

These days children arrive at school with little experience of being sung to and consequent ignorance of our heritage of nursery rhymes and songs. Their experience is more often television and they know the first two or three lines of jingles but no more. It is left to the teacher to remedy this and there is a wealth of suitable material to teach young children. Traditional songs from many lands have survived because they have catchy tunes, words that are easy to learn and are in a suitable range. These are the ingredients for a good choice of songs. Singing can become an important part of the school day, especially with the youngest children. You can plan the repertoire of songs with care, so as not just to fill in the odd moments at the end of the morning or during a wet playtime. Songs can be chosen for a purpose or sung for the sheer fun of singing. You can make the singing as musical as possible, and if a piano is not available, you can pitch in correctly using a chime bar, glockenspiel or xylophone. Many song books now give the name of the first note and these are marked on pitched percussion instruments.

Attitude is all important. Singing is fun, singing is important, singing is linked to many other subjects in the curriculum.

Some singing techniques

Sometimes a group of children are too inhibited to sing and I have found that it is possible to encourage them to use their voices freely with singing games. The voice is a very versatile instrument and you hear children in the playground shouting, screaming and squealing and these activities can be refined to suit your purpose.

When faced by a very reluctant class (age 7/8) I asked them to open their mouths and sing the highest note they could reach without screaming

> *'Make an 'aah' sound.'*
> *'Who can make the highest sound in the class?'*

They were only too delighted to join in.

> *'Now watch my hand. When it is high in the air, sing a high sound. When my hand is low towards the ground, sing as low as you can.'*

The children opened their mouths wide and sang.

> *'Now watch my hand very carefully and make your voice do what my hand asks it to do. Sing high notes and low notes. Let's change the sound and sing to 'oh'. We'll start low down.'*

A cacophony of low notes filled the room and the so called 'groaners' came into their own.

> *'Now I'm going to make patterns in the air with my hand. Can you sing the pattern? Don't worry about notes, try not to sing the same note as the person next to you but make your own note as round and beautiful as possible.'*

The notes were becoming more musical. I moved my hand from low to high, and from high to low.

> *'This time try to sing very quietly and again we'll change the sound. Try singing quietly to 'nah'.'*
> *'This time sing to 'meeh'.'*

The children were gaining in confidence as they realised what their voices were capable of. They had no words or rhythm to worry about, they were making high and low, and loud and quiet vocal sounds. We again discussed the concept of high and low, and found the low notes on the xylophone and chime bars. We discussed who could make the lowest note with their voices, and who the highest. Again two children who had thought of themselves as non-singers were proud to produce the lowest notes in the class. In our own time we moved up and down carrying our notes with us as high and as low as we could go.

Singing high and low

We went on to discuss simple mechanics of singing, that breath was all important. We played the game of taking in a deep breath and singing as many numbers as we could on one breath 1 2 3 4 5 6, and of course there was some cheating! We then discovered that the best way to breathe was from our diaphragms and if we lay flat on the floor this kept our shoulders still and encouraged diaphragmatic breathing which gave our voices much more support. This last game can only be done for a short time as children become self conscious and their breathing becomes erratic.

You can stress the importance of diction during singing by stressing the importance of the vowel sounds. It can be difficult to sing on consonants but it is obviously important to do so. We can play the game of opening our mouths and keeping our chins still and using the tongue to sing

    'lah lah lah' or *'te te te'*.

Humming is very beneficial and as most children smile when they hum this gives you the opportunity to point out that a relaxed smiling position helps to keep the pitch of the note they sing in tune as the sound comes forward using the cheek bones and head bones for resonance. This also improves the tone. You can encourage the child to sit or stand in a relaxed position, shoulders relaxed, chin in, not jutting out, and stretching their throats. You can make singing important by starting from silence, being counted in quietly either by a child or teacher. We need to learn to come in on the first note not half way through the first phrase, and to breathe just before the first note. A good finish is as important as a good start, finishing together perhaps with a slight slowing down of the tempo (known as *rallentando*).

Beautiful sound and good diction can be encouraged from a very early age. Encourage the children to note the difference between singing the vowels and consonants. Allow fairly free breathing, no gaps, but try not to breathe in the middle of a word, emphasising that they sing much as they would speak. Also become aware of the ways in which we use breathing and pitch in speech to communicate different messages. Singing is also important communication and if there is nothing to say there is nothing to sing.

Improving pitch

I am often asked by teachers what to do about the 'groaner'. There are very few children who are tone-deaf and I am convinced that children can be taught to improve their sense of pitch. Never discourage a child from singing. Often these children are the most enthusiastic and you can explain in a positive way that, just as it takes time to learn any skill, singing takes some people longer than others. With a good relationship this works well especially with younger children. These children can be encouraged to listen to themselves and to the notes they are required to sing and try to match them. You can also do some strategic placing of the less able between the more vocally able.

The creative approach gives children an opportunity to use their voices with confidence and this has a beneficial effect on the more formal class singing. Criticism may come from the child's peers as s/he gets older but very young children do not notice any lack of pitch, and the more uninhibited singing they can do, the better. The more we sing the better we become.

Teachers do not need operatic voices. Children prefer a gentler sound than a *bel canto* as I have found to my cost. It is rather discouraging to have the front row of children sitting with their fingers in their ears.

Using the voice in class

We can use our voices in many different ways. You can sing the register and ask the children to sing their reply. You can have a 'singing time' in the classroom when only sung communication is allowed. Children may be inhibited at first but when they discover that this is all for fun they will soon join in the game.

Teacher	*Catherine*	*soh*	*mi*
Child	*Ye-s*	*soh*	*mi*
Teacher	*Are you ready?*	*soh soh*	*mi* *doh*
Child	*Yes I am*	*mi mi*	*soh*

You can incorporate singing sounds into your creative writing and drama. A class of 5-year-olds was involved in a drama about the moon. We evolved a sung moon language in which the children put together syllables using the inflection in their voices to indicate questions and answers, happy, sad, angry and secret sounds. They became so involved that they were using their sung language in the playground much to the consternation of their dinner lady. A class of 6/7-year-olds was involved in a project on machines. They moved in groups like various different machines and used their voices to make the machine sounds. They went back to class and wrote down their machine sounds and then read them from their scores into a tape recorder.

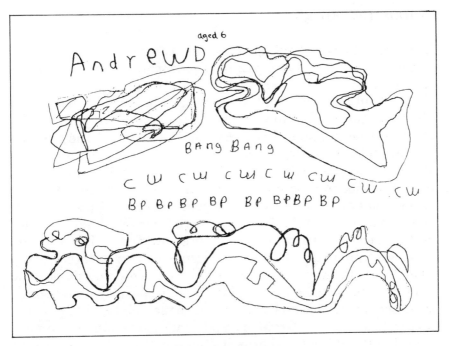

Sound patterns

Children use their voices to assist their movements in the playground and on observing this we incorporated the idea into movement lessons. When moving to make big long steps we found the quality of the movement improved if the child was allowed to make an appropriate sound to move to. Thus light quick movements have light quick sounds to accompany them, and so on. We can use our voices to imitate sounds we have heard and recall patterns of sound made by everyday objects and record them in our own way. The group of 6-year-olds working on a machines topic thought about washing machines and recalled the sound cycle, made the sounds with their voices and wrote them down in a sound sequence.

Switch on	*Click*
Fill	*Whishishishishishishish*
Heat	*Mm Mm Mm Mm Mm Mm*
Turn around	*Swish swish; Swish swish; Swish swish*
Empty	*Sssssssssssssss* (sucking teeth)
Fill	*Whish ish ish ish ish ish*
Heat	*Mm Mm Mm Mm Mm Mm*
Turn	*Swish swish; Swish swish; Swish swish*
Empty	*Sssssssssssssss* (sucking teeth)
Spin	*Zzzzzzzzzzzzzz* (like a bee)

Choosing songs

In a more formal singing lesson our choice of material is all important. There is now a wealth of good material and you should take time to search it out, (see pages 110—114). The songs you choose should be of the right range, usually between the note below middle C and around nine notes higher, although there will be children who can sing lower and higher than this. The children should understand the mood and content of the song and there should be an attractive tune and rhythm for them to enjoy. It is important not to choose a song merely because it fits a topic or theme you have selected. Children will learn a song just to please you if you have a good relationship with them but it never sounds quite as good as a song children really enjoy singing. It is also easy to underestimate the ability of children to learn a song they really like. After all, they learn very complicated pop song jingles and television themes and also sing very complicated playground songs, so we should match our choice of songs to their ability. Lizzie (age 3) is sung to at home by Grandma, and to my astonishment, she gave a good rendering of the chorus of 'Don't put your daughter on the stage Mrs Worthington' last term.

Children need a great deal of practice before they are able to sing and accompany themselves on instruments. With young children I tend to have one group singing and one group playing. We are asking a great deal of young children when we require them not only to remember and sing a song but also to remember an accompaniment. Older children find it easier after practice.

Teaching the song

The quality of singing often deteriorates when instruments are first introduced. The best way to teach a song is as a whole and unaccompanied. Sing the song through and ask the children to join in when they are able to do so. In every song there is a phrase which needs extra practice and this phrase can be sung in isolation and at a slower pace. Singing line by line is very boring. Necessary repetition needs careful handling. You can hum the tune, clap the rhythm and think the tune. You can sing the tune to 'lah'. You can sing (not shout) it as loudly as you can or sing it as quietly as you can. You can have one half of the class singing it to the other half, and vice versa. You can vary the teaching by warming up with exercises and then with an already known song before going back to the new song. It does no harm to point out to children that learning a song properly involves some work just like any other subject matter but that the learning can be pleasurable. When you know the words and tune, then you can add instruments and perhaps a second part.

You can also discuss the mood of the song and do some simple interpretation. When the piano or other accompaniment is added this also has to be learnt by the children and teacher. When performing a song it is a good idea to ask everyone to pay attention to the conductor (a teacher or child) who can bring the children in, and make sure that the tempo is kept and that the finish is clean. The teacher who cannot play the piano need not be put off as a taped accompaniment or a pitched percussion instrumental accompaniment can be used. A tuning fork is also useful to start the song off. You can teach songs relating to other areas of the curriculum. One of the most popular songs I teach at the moment is a tables calypso.

Once two is two
And two two's are four
And three two's are six
And four two's are eight
And five two's are ten
And six two's are twelve
And seven two's are always fourteen
Cha Cha Cha

Eight two's are sixteen
Nine two's are eighteen
Ten two's are twenty
Ten two's are twenty
Eleven two's are twenty two
Twelve two's are twenty four
That's how we add up the two's
Cha Cha Cha!

Music for tables calypso

You can teach repetitive songs, cumulative songs and songs with refrains. You can make sure that the children experience the numerous folk songs and popular songs of days gone by. Some of the most memorable concerts we have put on in every school in which I have taught have been Old Time Music Halls. Children enjoy the catchy tunes and the clever use of words, even though they do not fully understand all the nuances. A great deal of social history is taught incidentally through the songs. Not all songs we teach are happy but children can appreciate and enjoy the many beautiful, sad songs in our folklore and in the folklore of other countries. This familiarises them with the idea of different moods in music and the use of music to reflect or dispel moods.

You need to choose a variety of songs for your repertoire and always to be on the look-out for suitable material. The use of popular songs can build a bridge between the childen and us. Older children enjoy the challenge of more difficult songs with less obvious progressions and more complicated rhythm patterns but they also enjoy singing the easier songs just for the sheer joy of singing. In an atmosphere of praise and encouragement teachers' expectations can be high and if children are asked for just that little bit more effort, results can be surprising. Children enjoy singing their songs for other classes, for the headteacher or a local church or senior citizens home. These occasions reinforce the idea that singing is an important social activity capable of giving pleasure not only to ourselves but to others in the community. Also on these occasions a sense of performance including smart appearance, knowing where and how to stand and watching a conductor can be encouraged.

Simple part singing

You can teach simple rounds to introduce children to the idea of singing in harmony. Encourage the children to sing quietly enough to hear the harmonies they are creating. You can use singing games to introduce singing in parts.

Simple sol-fa is not difficult to learn and with the help of pitched percussion instruments you can sing chord tunes. You can divide the class into three groups. Then choose a chord, perhaps **C** major

soh **G**
mi **E**
doh **C**

Give each group one of the three chime bars. In each group, one child plays the chime bar and the others sing that note. Point to each group in turn so that each group plays and sings its note. Then point to each group again and this time the children of all three groups keep repeating their notes. This then achieves a simple harmony.

Soundscapes

It is not always necessary for groups to harmonize in the traditional way. You can sing note clusters dividing the class into groups according to their preference.

low   middle   high.

The children can be conducted either by a teacher or by a member of the group. The conductor can choose a vowel sound for them to sing and vary the sound by giving previously agreed signals for tempo, dynamics and pitch. The children can choose notes to sing that are comfortably within their own vocal range. You can use a word or phrase and break it up into a pattern of vowel and consonant sounds sung within the bounds of sound and silence, quiet and loud, quick and slow to give a shape to your 'soundscape'.

One of the most recent soundscapes we composed was with a class of 10/11-year-olds and was called 'Rainforest'. After a great deal of discussion we decided how to sing the sounds making up the word 'Rainforest', whether to sing them loudly or quietly, fast or slow, or whether to move from low to high, loud to quiet etc. The score was then written out and each part sung in turn. Pupils chose a note which they could sing comfortably and which was different from their neighbour's. One of the pupils pointed to each part and the rest followed the pointer and sang each part in turn from 1–9. The blocks of sound at the end were sung again very loudly on notes of individual choice.

Rainforest

Voices only

1 *R r r r r r r r r r r r r*
   (ff)   (mf)

2 *ai*_____
   (sustained on one breath:
   1 2 3 4 5 6 7 8)

3 (p, high) *n n n n n n n*
   (f, low) *n n n n n n n*

4 *R - ai - n   R - ai - n   R - ai - n*
   (ff and sung on note of choice)

5 *f f f f f f f f f f f f*
   (fast, unvoiced)

6 *o*_____
(moving up the scale chosen from
loud to quiet)

7 *or or or or or or*
(mf)

8 *e*_____*st*   *e*_____*st*
   (1 2 3 4 5)   (1 2 3 4 5)

9 *rain   forest   rain   forest   rain   forest*

☐   ☐   ☐   ☐   ☐   ☐

(1   2 3   1   2 3   1   2 3)
(blocks of sound)

Composing songs

Children can be encouraged to use their voices as a means of
composition. Small children will sing their own songs to the class
without inhibition and if this is encouraged, other children in the
group will also try. Many of these songs are long and meandering
but if the teacher has time and patience to listen it is very
worthwhile. Sensitive intervention can cut down the repetition and
often produce a song the whole class can learn. With confidence
this skill improves and children eventually sing their contribution
to a class story or project. During a story session a class of 7-year-
olds with their classteacher were making up a story about a lonely
snowman and when asked what the snowman would do next,
Nicholas said 'He may sing a song to cheer himself up.' 'What do
you think he would sing?' asked the teacher.

Nicholas sang the following song.

Shuffling along on the cold dusty street
I'm crying and crying today
I'm only a poor sorrowful man
I'm lonely because I've no friends.

Nicholas' song

Nicholas repeated the song, note perfect when we taped the finished story the following day. Songs can be part of a story and can give small children something to contribute to the telling of a story. A suitable song can be learnt and sung at appropriate intervals. Many examples of this are found in '*Sing a Song*' Books 1 and 2 by Wendy Bird.

Composing songs is not as difficult as it is sometimes thought. A class of 11-year-olds composed the following contemporary carol. We had been discussing the material aspect of Christmas and the lack of religious emphasis. They suggested the appropriate phrases and after lively discussion we put the words together. Emma sang the first two lines and we progressed from there.

Christmas Song

(Played on descant recorder with tambour)

D   G   G   A B   C B   A

The streets are bright on Christmas night

B   G G   A F# G

With Christmas trees and stars

D   G   G   A   B C B   A

The doors are decked with holly wreaths

B   G   G A F# G

The roads are full of cars

A B C D D E E   D

The people hurry to and fro

C   B   A   G B   A

With bags and bags of things

D G G A B C A   B G G   A F# G

O what do we remember when of these things we sing?

```
D    G   G   A   B  CB A
|    |   |   |   |  ⌐⌐ |
```
When presents are given and taken

```
B G  G   A  F#   G
| ⌐⌐ |   |  |    |
```
O do we stop to think

```
D  GG   A A   CB    A
|  ⌐⌐   ⌐⌐   ⌐⌐    |
```
Of Jesus in a stable cold

```
B     G   G   A  F#   G
|     |   |   |  |    |
```
Midst all this food and drink

```
A  B  C   D   D  E E  D
|  |  |   |   |  ⌐⌐ |
```
Of all the Christmases of old

```
C   B A   G B   A
|   | |   | |   |
```
Of shepherds and of kings

```
D  G  G  A B  C   B A
|  |  ⌐⌐⌐⌐ |  |   | |
```
Do we remember all mankind

```
B    G   G A F#   G
|    |   ⌐⌐ |    |
```
When bells begin to ring?

The following song was composed by Alexa (9-years-old) on her recorder.

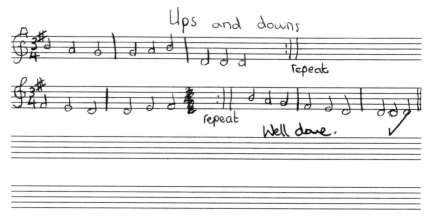

Alexa's song

Some songs may have only three or four notes and can be very short. They can be composed for their own sake and either words or tune can come first. Children may compose a tune for a poem they have enjoyed or to add to a theme of an assembly or a drama. In my experience children learn their own songs very quickly and achieve a great deal of satisfaction from their compositions.

Balloon song

You can encourage children to use their voices in a variety of ways to add another dimension to work in: dance, drama, language and communication subjects. Singing can develop into a lifelong interest and leisure activity and is well worth doing for its own sake.

2 Making and using a collection of percussion instruments

Most primary school teachers who opt to take music, are expected to introduce children to percussion instruments. Unless they attended an enlightened college they have had very little experience of playing percussion instruments themselves. In my own case I found myself learning with the children but the problem was where to start! In my first school we found a cupboard full of rusting cymbals, and old tambourines and triangles, so over the years we bought a selection of new instruments. We found that one or two well made instruments of good quality are worth more than several cheaper ones. It is from these instruments that children will learn to discriminate between good and inferior sounds. A basic school collection could be

Unpitched
  Tambourines
  Triangles of different sizes
  Snare drums
  Tambours
  Small drums
  Bongo drums
  Bass drums
  Indian bells
  Cymbals (including one 18 inch)
  Chinese beaters
  Castanets
  Maracas
  Ubo
  Swannee whistle

Pitched
  Set of chime bars
  Glockenspiels, soprano and alto
  Xylophones, soprano, alto and bass

Also desirable are: various beaters capable of producing a wide range of tone colour, for example with wool, felt and hard rubber heads; and side drum sticks and brushes.

All this more expensive apparatus can be provided slowly over the years possibly through fund-raising activities.

A sound table or corner can be provided without involving a great deal of expense. Noise level can be a problem but this is determined by what you choose to provide and how you control the activities in the sound corner. Initially small children will try to make as much noise as possible, but with supervision and purpose, a sound corner need not cause any more noise than a Wendy house or woodwork corner. A few instruments can be put out at a time, carefully chosen to keep the noise level acceptable, without inhibiting the children's enthusiasm and curiosity. In my present school, we provided a selection of instruments for the nursery class and eventually even the 3-year-olds were playing the instruments carefully and discussing their findings.

Lizzie	*'My drum makes a big sound'*
Edward	*'My tambourine is all shaky'*
Lizzie	*'My drum sound is louder than yours'*
Robert	*'I can hear the drum if I play soft'*
Lizzie	*'I'd rather play a loud tune'*

You can also provide a sound corner and place less conventional sound-producing objects alongside the more conventional percussion instruments, for example

Egg cartons
Metal dustbin lid
Pieces of corrugated plastic (rough edges covered by elastoplast)
Metal sheets
Cartons containing peas, lentils, beans, rice
Box of paper, newspaper, tissues, sugar paper, foil
Plant pots of various sizes
Egg slicer
Cheese grater
Selection of plastic and cardboard boxes
Box of elastic bands of various thicknesses
Box of nails of varying lengths
Box of spoons, sticks, pencils to act as beaters

The sound frame

We discovered that objects made a more interesting and resonant sound if suspended and we tried several ways of suspending them safely. A clothes airer was too flimsy and an old bookcase with shelves removed fell over, so we searched catalogues and the headmistress discovered a frame (about $1\frac{1}{2}$ m high and $1\frac{1}{2}$ m wide) originally meant for art display. This became our sound frame. We hung our sound-producing objects in various ways, sometimes in sets, for example

> Set of high sounds
> Set of low sounds
> Set of loud sounds
> Set of quiet sounds
> Set of hard sounds

We sometimes hung objects varying from small to large, from left to right on the frame, as in more conventional instruments. We hung flower pots, nails of different sizes, wooden spoons and our precious metal dustbin lid which in these days of plastic bins are difficult to find.

Children entered into the task of finding sound-producing objects in their homes or on the way to school, and objects such as the egg slicer, on which David (age 6) discovered that he could pluck a tune, arrived daily. After an initial period of distrust, one caretaker arrived with a large plunger which he said made an interesting sound on the floor. The children discovered many facts about the properties of sound. They discovered that large objects made lower sounds than smaller ones and that some materials were more resonant than others. We listened to the sound made when the object was suspended and able to vibrate and not 'stopped' by a hand. We discussed the highest sounds, the loudest sounds, the quietest sounds, etc especially when organising the sets. The children played their own patterns of sound, playing on the sound frame after a period of experimentation.

A visiting H.M.I. became very interested in all this work and took a small group of children round the frame and gave them the following tasks.

1 Play your sound pattern
2 Play it, rest it, then play it again
3 Play it, then play it backwards
4 Play it, think it, then play it again

He was surprised how well the children carried out these tasks, proving that their playing was structured and not just 'messing about'. He also taught me a lesson in how to structure their experimental playing.

Sounds in the environment

It soon becomes obvious to children that any sound is of interest and worth investigation. Pencils on a table make a different sound from pencils on a tin, hands on the PE mats make a different sound from hands on a tiled floor, beaters on dustbin lids make a different sound from beaters on desks, and different beaters make different sounds on the same objects. Why? This was the question and this leads into work on the physics of sound (Chapter 5).

One day we took a class of children (age 6/7) equipped with sticks and beaters to play in the playground. The children found some interesting sounds.

Playing a tree in the playground

Playing a wall

Mary	'If I run this metal rod against the grid it makes a jagged sound'
John	'When I play the bars of the ladder on the climbing frame with the same beater they all make the same sound'
Teacher	'Why do you think that is?'
John	'Is it because the rungs are the same size?'
Teacher	'Yes, and the same material. And the beater is the same, as you said. Try hitting them with different beaters'
Naina	'If I play the railings with a hard beater they make a louder sound than with a soft headed beater'
Mary	'I get a louder sound with this stick on the floor than with a soft beater'
John	'I get a louder sound if I hit the floor really hard'

Sounds discovered in the classroom

The language of sound

During all these activities the children are learning the language of sound. You can teach the physics of sound very simply to children who understand the differences between high and low, fast and slow, quiet and loud, continuous and interrupted. A child needs to know the language in order to express her/his findings correctly. Physical activities reinforce these findings. Later on this knowledge can be translated into the correct musical terms:

> Pitch or frequency (high/low)
> Duration (long/short)
> Intensity (loud/quiet)
> Speed (fast/slow)
> Harmony (sounds together)

With these principles in mind the child's experience can be guided into some kind of pattern of organised sound so that experimentation is not haphazard but a way of guiding the child's own interest and enthusiasm into an awareness and appreciation of the sounds around and how they are produced. Most children are bombarded by a barrage of sound both at home and at school. It is a rare moment when there is total quiet. When asked by the teacher, a group of 8-year-olds said that the only time there was quiet in their environment was if they woke in the middle of the night. Apart from this time, they lived at home with a background noise of television or radio and personal stereos, and taped music in the car or supermarket and in most shops. Children have developed the facility of 'switching off'. We can teach them to tune in again. We know from experience that children who become aware of the natural sounds around them become more selective and interested in the sounds in their environment, and discriminating and capable of organising their environment in a way which satisfies them — perhaps even turning off the television, the personal stereo etc.

Composing sound patterns

Children can be taught to compose their own sound patterns using the objects around them, and ordering sound in this way demands as much sensitivity to texture and shape as composition using more conventional instruments. A teacher does not need a conventional musical education to encourage this work. A child can be taught to discriminate, to change and to limit, by a teacher sensitive to that child's own compositions. Working from this base of confidence, achievement is enriching and stimulating. I have seen many examples of teachers who have tried out this kind of approach and become very excited by the results. They express great surprise at what children of all ages can achieve when given the opportunity and encouragement to compose using sounds produced by 'junk' material or ordinary objects. Some of the compositions are very complex, and ingenious ways are found of recording the sound patterns or compositions.

Sounds in the classroom

The following are graphic notation scores composed by 7/9-year-olds using conventional instruments and working in pairs without teacher supervision.

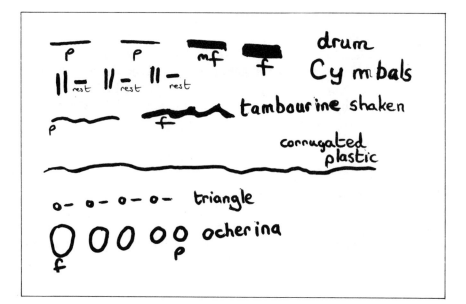

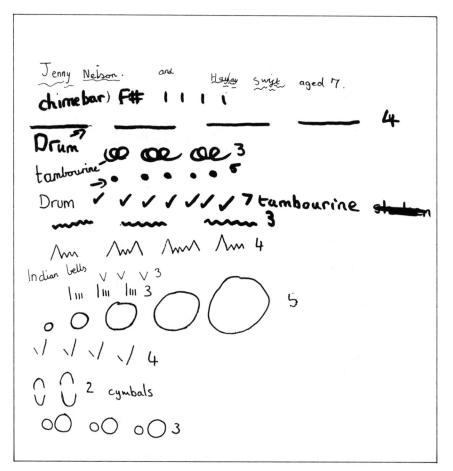

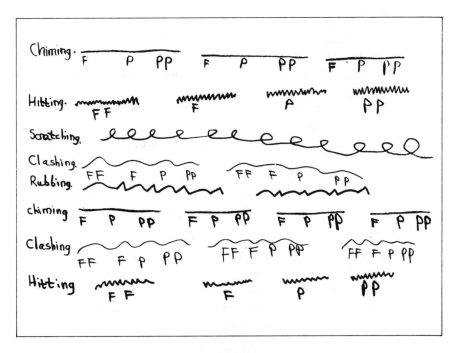

I am not suggesting that work with conventional instruments should grow out of work with junk but that both kinds of work should continue side by side. Also that creative music does not need expensive instruments. Ideally children should look for the sound required. In a rich environment of sound-producing objects, they should choose an instrument, whether it is conventional or not, because it produces the sound required.

Using conventional instruments

As a starting point, look at one instrument, for example a tambourine. Very young children first learn its name and then look at its construction.

What shape is it?
What is it made of?
What sounds can it produce?
How many different sounds can we make?
Can we made high sounds?
     low sounds?
     loud sounds?
     quiet sounds?
     sounds that go on and on?
     sounds that have a quiet time between them?

Show the children how to hold the tambourine properly, without putting their fingers through the hole designed for ribbons. They should hold it so that the thumb is over the skin and is therefore free to stop the vibration of the skin if necessary. Demonstrate a way of hitting it making your free hand into a 'snake's head' and tapping the skin on the centre to produce a resonant sound. The children can then experiment with a tambourine held in the hand and compare its more resonant sound with that obtained when it is played flat on the table. Running their thumbs round the edge of the skin will produce a roll. The level at which we approach techniques depends on the age of the child. With little ones I believe that it is attitude that we are teaching by our own example.

An instrument is fun to play but is precious, and whilst you can produce a loud sound you do not do it by bashing or banging. This applies equally to less conventional instruments. We once found three beer cans that when hit produced a primary triad. These were as precious as the most expensive conventional instrument and were treated as such. In one school because of the numbers on roll I had to move out of my music room into the entrance hall. We left all the percussion instruments on display in the hall and 230 children passed them several times a day. In two terms we had one drum holed by an over-enthusiastic 7-year-old. Whilst I would encourage children to play an instrument however they wish, they are expected to produce a good sound and are taught from the age of three that instruments are precious and should be respected for the present and the future.

Beginning to score

A class of 5-year-olds working with tambourines produced the following ways of playing.

Hitting
Tapping with fingers
Shaking
Flicking
Tapping the bells
Scratching the skin
Rubbing across the back with hand

We discussed whether these sounds were continuous or whether they had a 'quiet bit' in between. We discussed whether the sound went up and down. We found out that sounds became louder as we hit harder. We thought about how we could write the sounds down and drew the pattern by the side of our list. We then decided to compose a pattern for the whole class to play together and wrote it out on a large piece of paper. We started from silence and had to practise to ensure that everyone with a tambourine counted correctly and watched the score.

This was the result.

4	hits	○ ○ ○ ○
6	taps	| | | | | |
5	flicks	✓ ✓ ✓ ✓ ✓
8	taps	• • • • • • • •
3	scratches	○ ○ ○
4	rubs	⟋⟋⟋⟋
1	large shake	∿∿∿∿

Children can eventually learn to work alone or in pairs choosing their own instruments and composing their own sound patterns. A 6-year-old boy, Paul, working with a tambourine produced the following pattern

6 hits	○ ○ ○ ○ ○ ○
a long jangle	∿∿∿∿∿∿∿∿∿∿∿
1 hit on each side	○ ○
a long jingle	∿∿∿∿∿∿∿∿∿∿∿∿
hit rest hit etc	○ ⌣ ○ ⌣ ○ ⌣

Paul did not realise that he had used the correct terminology for 'a silence' in music. He just thought that as he was having a rest that is what he would write.

In teaching the more formal aspects of music we can begin from what the child knows already. In its simplest form, the theory is very logical and most teachers, especially in primary schools, can approach music as they do many other subjects and learn through teaching the children.

Teaching rhythm

The most difficult concept for children is the idea of rhythm. A pulse or beat, determined by a conductor or by the music itself, which sets a regular or irregular pattern until the music is finished, is a difficult concept for children to grasp. They can soon listen for the heavy beat in a piece of music and counting from there, decide how many beats there are in a bar but it is the breaking up of the pulse into so many different rhythms with rests of differing lengths that is hard to imagine. I have found the earlier you start to make children conscious of their own body rhythms, the better. When walking, running, skipping, hopping, or jumping, young children can become conscious of the regular rhythm of their movements. You can accompany these activities with a percussion instrument, for example using a drum or chords on a piano to help them differentiate between the different rhythmic patterns. I am certain that some children have an innate sense of rhythm but others have to be taught. If children have plenty of experience in movement by listening to their own pulse or heart beat and playing it on a percussion instrument or by becoming aware of the rhythmic nature of a ticking clock, or chopping wood, hammering a nail, vacuuming the house, rowing a boat, they can soon come to terms with rhythm.

With young children you can play or clap the first line of a nursery rhyme or well known song for them to recognise stressing the loud or heavy beat.

   | ⌣ | ⌣
Baa baa black sheep
   | ⌣   ⌣ |
Have you any wool?

You can then play a game with the class asking one child to tap out the rhythm of the first line of a song for everyone to recognise. You can also say well known poems or nursery rhymes clapping or playing percussion instruments only on the heavy beat.

   | ⌣ | ⌣ | |
Incey Wincey spider
    | | ⌣ |
Climbed up the spout

You also need to use poems and songs where the off beat comes first, for example

  ⌣ | ⌣ |
By yon bonnie banks

These activities introduce children to the loud and quiet pulses in music and every time you sing or play recorded music you can draw their attention to the beat. This leads on to discussion of bar lines and time signatures. One very popular game with children is to play their name pattern.

Shil-pi Hai   *Robert Jones*   *Vincent Cheong*

You can encourage the children to compose short rhythmic patterns to play on unpitched percussion instruments.

The children can also work in pairs using instruments or body sounds, for example clicking, clapping, stamping etc for question and answer phases. Words are not always necessary and the patterns can stand alone.

Question | | ⊓ | ?
Answer | | | | .

Workcards can be made and put into the sound or music corner for the children to play rhythmic patterns on instruments or with body sounds.

walk   *walk*   *walk*   *walk*

run run *run run* *walk*   *walk*

run run *run run* *run run* *walk*

The children's names can be put into sets depending on how many pulses they contain. At this stage children tend to count the syllables and ignore the stresses.

Jane   *Ahmed*   *Samantha*   *Gunapria*
Chan   *Mary*   *Christopher*
James   *Hannah*   *Harriet*
              Shaanti

Names can be put together to form a rhythmic pattern for the child to play

Jessica Mary

On a music course in Hampshire we were encouraged to help children to understand the different note values by using the names of drinks. This worked very well

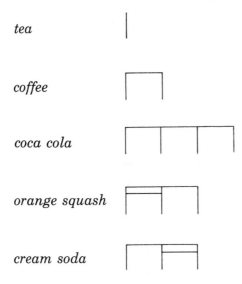

tea

coffee

coca cola

orange squash

cream soda

The problem can be teaching that each of these rhythms takes up only one pulse. Children need to listen to rhythm in all kinds of music to be aware of rhythm, to hear and listen and move to it and to see it in some form of notation. Although this comes after young children have had plenty of experience in listening and moving, and learning to rest when the sound stops, they need to feel and move to the pulse and to sing it before they attempt to write it down.

Awareness of pitch

We often assume that children understand the words they use so glibly. As a young teacher I was horrified by the result when a visiting inspector asked my class if they knew the difference between high and low. The children were 5-years-old and when asked to close their eyes and listen to notes played on the piano and xylophone and respond by stretching high for a high note and crouching low for a low note a significant number of children got it wrong. They knew the words but did not understand the concept. Since then I have done a great deal of work with children relating to high and low.

Is it high or low?

We collect lists of objects producing high sounds and those producing low sounds. We move like high and low objects, and from low to high and vice versa. Experience of low sounds can be gained better from a bass xylophone than from a treble, and the whole range of recorders should provide opportunities for young children to make and hear a full spectrum of sounds. You can play the lowest notes on the piano, listen to the double bass or cello or to a bass drum and point out the lowest notes in recorded music. With a lot of experience of these sounds you can then introduce work on comparative pitch:

high   higher   highest
low   lower   lowest

Children's attention can be drawn to everyday objects whose sound goes from low to high and vice versa, for example a food mixer, a spin dryer, a kettle whistle.

Physical activity is usually children's first response to music. Using this response, their ears and their voices, and through creative work with all kinds of sound-producing objects including conventional percussion instruments, you can try to ensure that children understand the musical concepts you are teaching. A good teacher, sensitive to the children's needs and interests, does not need to be a great musician to foster an interest in this work. Many primary school teachers, myself included, teach and include art in all their topics and activities. We do not have to be great artists to provide a suitable environment for children to work in. The appropriate tools of the trade need to be available and in good working order.

Teachers' experience and common sense can guide, encourage and help children without too much interference or imposition of their own ideas. This is possible too with the teaching of music. I hope that in this book some ideas will appeal to the different strengths we all have, and will encourage the non-specialist to create an environment in which children will use sound and music to enrich their activities in the same way that they use art.

Awareness of dynamics

Loud and quiet is comparatively easy for a child to understand. Most of them have been told to be quiet all their lives. The aim is not to encourage a child to make a noise but to make a sound constructively and, even harder, to make a quiet sound not to please an adult but because a quiet sound is required to make a pattern of sound.

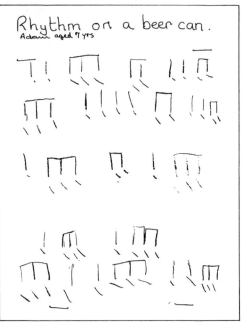

Rhythm on a beer can

You can encourage a child to move quietly. 5-year-old Alan described himself as moving 'like a secret'. We can play instruments quietly, getting louder, or loudly getting quieter and show the relevant markings

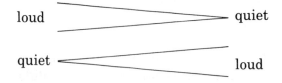

You can go out into the playground and listen for loud and quiet sounds and make lists. 6-year-old Lucy with her ear to the grass said that she could hear a worm moving. When we play instruments in groups it is a good thing to encourage loud as well as quiet playing even if it is sometimes hard on the teacher's ears. You can play records at their proper level and not as background noise.

Duration of sounds

Children find the concept of long and short sounds fairly easy to grasp although when finding the largest sound possible on a variety of percussion instruments they may play several sounds in quick succession as one long sound. A good exercise is to sit a group or class of children in a circle each with a percussion instrument and ask for one sound from each child. Each child waits for the previous sound to die away before playing her/his sound. Those instruments playing a long sound soon become obvious.

Simple techniques

Most primary school teachers who opt to take music have little or no experience in playing the instruments. Some enlightened colleges include the use of percussion instruments in their general music course but not many do so. It will be easier for teachers to teach percussion if they familiarise themselves with basic techniques. In Hampshire we were very fortunate in having a professional percussionist who came into school to demonstrate. It is possible that the peripatetic percussion teacher would be happy to come into the primary school to start pupils off correctly.

The correct technique produces the best sound and is often the easiest way for small children to begin. Experimenting with the different effects produced by different positions or hand shapes will draw children's attention to the quality of sound and to the most effective technique. For example, when holding a tambourine, the child should not put the thumb into the hole on the rim as that is primarily for ribbons. Making the hand into a 'snake's head' when tapping the tambourine produces the most resonant sound (much better than a flat hand) and the sound is better if the tambourine is held, rather than played on the ground. Quite young children can manage a finger trill, made by running fingers and thumb round the edge of the skin to play the bells.

When playing a triangle, it should be held with finger and thumb free to stop the sound when necessary. The correct way to hold a beater is as if you were shaking hands with it. To play a xylophone, chime bars or glockenspiel properly, it is necessary to use both hands. So right from the beginning, it is important to get children to hold a beater in each hand, even if they actually only use one of them at first. These instruments make a fuller sound when hit in the middle of the bar. Single chime bars and claves are better when balanced on the hand rather than clasped. Bongo drums should be played as though you have received an electric shock on touch. As most playing comes from the wrist then it is a good idea to give the children practice in using wrists.

It is up to the teacher to keep the instruments in good repair and in some kind of order with two suitable beaters nearby. There is nothing more frustrating for a child than not to be able to find a beater or to have to untangle triangle strings or be given a glockenspiel with some of the bars missing. These previous techniques are for conventional playing of instruments. There is a place for experimentation, for example cymbals played with violin bows. One of the most successful instruments I have used was an old piano with both fronts off so that all the strings were exposed. We 'doctored' these with rubbers, nails, spoons, pencils and strummed the thick strings with a loud pedal on, to produce thunder sounds. When we had a space topic with a class of 7-year-olds we produced some very interesting space music.

Even when experimenting with sounds it is a good thing to teach some basic percussion technique. Small children tend to attack musical instruments with great enthusiasm and whilst you do not in any way wish to inhibit this approach a certain degree of control produces a more musical sound. You can demonstrate to children that a satisfactory loud musical sound can be produced without destroying an instrument! Indeed, most children obtain great satisfaction from producing controlled sound which matches the mood of their composition. I subscribe strongly to the idea that every instrument is precious and should be treated as such even if it is an empty beer can we are playing. If this attitude is learnt by the children then we need not lock our instruments and sound-producing materials away in cupboards to be brought out on Friday afternoons but can leave them freely available for children to use in order to add another dimension to all their work in school.

3 Music and language

Music is in itself a language through which we can communicate our feelings and perceptions. We do this by making sounds and by listening and interpreting the sounds of others. There is a need to identify the sounds and patterns described in this particular language both when making music or listening to it and for this we need to learn the necessary vocabulary. Children have to be able to demonstrate musically the difference between fast and slow, loud and quiet, high and low. They have to be able to make use of rhythm, echo, repetition, phrase and shape, leaps, gradual building, getting faster and slower and all the variations of these terms. Here you have a framework in which to teach musical concepts. Children enjoy translating these terms into physical activity. They can move to a fast drum beat or a series of slow chords on a piano or beats on percussion. They can listen to a piece of music and describe the shape of it with their hands or whole bodies. They can work in pairs with percussion to play question and answer games. As far as possible the teacher can use conventional musical terminology to describe the music they are making or listening to. Here are some of the more common terms.

piano, written	*p*	quiet
	mp	quieter
	pp	very quiet
forte, written	*f*	loud
	mf	louder
	ff	very loud
rallentando or *ral*		slowing down
crescendo	⟨	getting louder
diminuendo	⟩	getting quieter
pizzicato		plucked

da capo	from the beginning
treble	high
bass	low
staff or stave	5 lines on which the music is written
bar lines	lines across the stave dividing the note values to provide the time indicated
time signature $\left(\text{eg } \frac{2}{2} \ \frac{4}{4} \ \frac{6}{8} \ \frac{3}{4} \right)$	a kind of fraction in which the number at the top is the number of beats in the bar and the number at the bottom shows the kind of note used for the beat of the music
key signature	instead of writing sharps and flats by each note as required to produce the major or minor scales they are written at the beginning as a 'key signature'
scale	major scale is eight sounds in alphabetical order with a semitone between the 3rd and 4th and the 7th and 8th and a tone between the other steps or degrees

Children usually enjoy learning the correct musical terminology and, if taught incidentally, and wherever appropriate, soon become familiar with it. When children are given the opportunity to listen to, and create music, they feel and demonstrate all these terms without knowing the correct vocabulary. It is our task as teachers to intervene where possible to teach the correct terms and encourage their use. This is evident when children are creating their own music and attempting to write a score (see Chapter 4) or listening to a song or recorded music and attempting to explain what they feel the music is doing. Simon (age 6), when listening to 'The Aquarium' from Saint-Saëns' 'Carnival of the Animals' said 'The sound is all darty and rushing about'. He proceeded to move his hands fast like fishes. Later when listening to 'The Cuckoo at the Edge of the Forest' Mary said 'That instrument's just right for a bird. I can see it in my head'. The teacher was able to explain simply that the way the music was written painted these pictures for them and terms like fast, high, smooth, flowing, came into use.

Children's general vocabulary can be greatly extended during musical activities. On the more formal side from very early experience they learn the names of percussion and other instruments and their components, for example a piano, keys, pedals, music stand, etc. They learn the titles and words of songs, names of composers, some forms of music, for example concerto, symphony, sonata, opera. They learn the names of the instruments of the orchestra, and some related terms, for example conductor, baton, podium. They learn the names of other groups of musicians, for example choir, group, trio, quartet, quintet, sextet, chamber group. They learn the names of different types of music from different countries and different periods. For example Jamaican reggae, rap, folk songs, Indian music, music from our own culture, madrigals, rounds, different kinds of popular music.

Communication through music and sound

We can compose sound stories with one child writing the story and another one or two collecting the sound effects or we can write a class story and the whole class can provide the sound effects. A great deal of useful discussion takes place during the choice of instruments or sound-producing objects as to which is the best sound to include in our stories. A group of 5/6-year-olds on a particularly sunny morning in January produced the following poem with sound effects

A Winter Morning

Dragons breathe like smoke from my mouth
Frost sparkling in the red sun (*triangle* × *6*)
Freezing cold wind (*voices*)
Shivering and shaking (*maracas* × *5*)
Slipping and sliding (*guiro* × *4*)
Frosty grass and pavements (*Indian bell* × *2*)
Pond hard and icy (*G chime bar* × *3*)
Iced-up cars and windows (*cymbals scraped round* × *3*)
Bare silver branches of trees (*glockenspiel G A Bb* × *2*)
Round red winter sun (*cymbals clashed* × *1*)

A teacher who draws the children's attention to the soundscape in which they live will find that they enjoy describing the sounds of which they become aware either in school or at home. A class of 5-year-olds became very agitated when describing a new supermarket which had just opened down the road from the school. It was the noise of the place they found most disturbing. The teacher wrote down what they said about it.

Jenny   *'I don't like it. It is very noisy and crashy. The music is too loud. The people talk loudly. It is very light and it makes me frightened.'*

James   *'I think a giant lives there. I can hear him talking. I don't like the noises. The trolleys pinch me. The music goes on and on.'*

Jane   *'I like the music. I don't like all the people. They push my mum and shout all the time.'*

Maria   *'Loud and noisy and bright and lots of people. It's crashy and high up.'*

Older children write more complex sound stories and find complicated ways of drawing their sound effects. The following two sound stories were written by children, the first by 11-year-olds in a class of 28, the second by 7-year-olds in a class of 25.

Story 1

The spaceship was launched (*voices*). It glided through space (*glockenspiel C E D F G C × 4*). It passed the planet Mars (*bass drum × 6*), it went past the galaxy of the Milky Way (*plastic pipe whirred round*), past the Great Bear (*tambourine shaken*), past Jupiter (*bongo drums* ⊓ |) and landed on Saturn (*cymbals*). The two spacemen climbed out and walked through the atmosphere (*cymbals scraped round*). An alien figure appeared. It was green and ugly. It had 7 eyes (*triangle × 7*), 3 large ears (*tambourine × 3*) and when it spoke it made a strange clattering noise (*tin cans*). It beckoned to the spacemen and led them into a cave. Inside, strange birds flew around (*recorders blown freely*) and peculiar looking animals moved threateningly towards the men (*drums × 10*). The men took fright and moved as quickly as they could back to the spaceship. The animals and birds chased after them but they were too quick (*recorders, drums freely*). They just managed to launch the spaceship leaving the planet behind (*cymbals*).

Story 2

David and Richard went sailing on the ocean in their new dinghy. A great wind blew up (*treble xylophone glissando*) and the boat capsized (*cymbal*). The boys floated into the water, down and down (*bass xylophone*). Suddenly they saw a strange creature coming towards them (*psaltery*). It was a sea witch. She had red eyes (*maracas*) and green bedraggled hair (*psaltery*). Her hands were long with pointed nails (*tambour*). Her feet were webbed (*uvo*). She floated towards them and chanted a curious spell:

Nose of swordfish (*beer tins, Chinese beaters*)
Mackerel bones (*tulip beaters, claves, xylophone with sticks*)
Octopus eyes (*sharps and flats on glockenspiel*)
Skin of shark (*guiro*)
Turn these boys into wizards.

The witch wanted them to help her to wreck ships. The spell worked in the wrong way. All the fish in the spell became the boys' friends and came to their rescue and chased the sea witch away.

Swordfish (*guiro*)
Mackerel (*claves, swannee whistle*)
Octopus (*triangles, tambourine shaken*)
Shark (*bass drum*)

Children enjoy going on a listening walk. After such an outing a class of 4/5-year-olds described their walk in a class story.

Heavy feet on the school yard (*clop, clop, clop, clop, clop, clop*)
The gate creaked (*eeeeeeeeeeeeeeeee*)
We closed it with a BANG
We walked on the hard pavement (*clop, clop, clop, clop, clop clop*)
We walked on the grass (*swish, swish, swish, swish, swish, swish*)
We saw a dog and it barked at us (*woof woof*)
We heard some traffic (*brum, brum, brum*)
We heard some birds (*cr, cr; tck tck; tweet tweet*)
We laughed and chattered (*children's voices*)
We walked on gravel +++++++++++++++++
We stood by the pond (*lap, lap*)
The ducks quacked (*quack, quack*)
We saw a coot land (*whoosh*)
Johnny walked in some water (*splash*)
We enjoyed our walk

It is possible to compose a story using sound effects only. The following one was composed by a group of 6/8-year-olds.

1 Crash of glass
2 Running feet (quiet in trainers)
3 Police whistle
4 Heavy feet running
5 Hard breathing coming closer
6 Sound of fall
7 Sound of scuffle

8 Police car coming nearer
9 More scuffles
10 Police car starting then fading into distance
11 Sounds of sweeping glass

Creative writing using sounds and recorded music as a stimulus

You can choose a suitable piece of music and play a short part of it and then ask the children to either tell or write a story or paint a picture describing what they think the music is about or how the music makes them feel. This can be a piece of programme music which tells a story or specifically describes a situation or it can be a more abstract piece of music. If you do not tell the children what the composer had in mind but leave it to the children's imagination you can achieve some very interesting results. You are reinforcing the concept of mood music which evokes certain emotions. Here is a list of music which is useful for this activity but there are many more.

The Sorcerer's Apprentice Dukas
Till Eulenspiegel's Merry Pranks Richard Strauss
The Lark Ascending (for violin and orchestra) Vaughan Williams
Swan Lake Tchaikovsky
Romeo and Juliet (Overture) Tchaikovsky
The Planets Holst
A Midsummer Night's Dream Britten
Noye's Fludde Britten
Visage Berio
The Pines of Rome Respighi
L'Après midi d'un Faune Debussy
Carnival of the Animals Saint-Saëns
Peter and the Wolf Prokofiev
Pictures at an Exhibition Musorgsky
Capriccio Espagnol Rimsky Korsakov
The Magic Flute (Overture) Mozart
The Thieving Magpie (Overture) Rossini
William Tell (Overture) Rossini
The Firebird Stravinsky

A class of 9/10-year-olds listened to the slow movement of the *Eine kleine Nachtmusik* by Mozart. Their teacher played the music to them without telling them anything about it and they then painted a scene suggested to them by the music. The list of paintings included:

LIBRARY, UNIVERSITY COLLEGE CHESTER

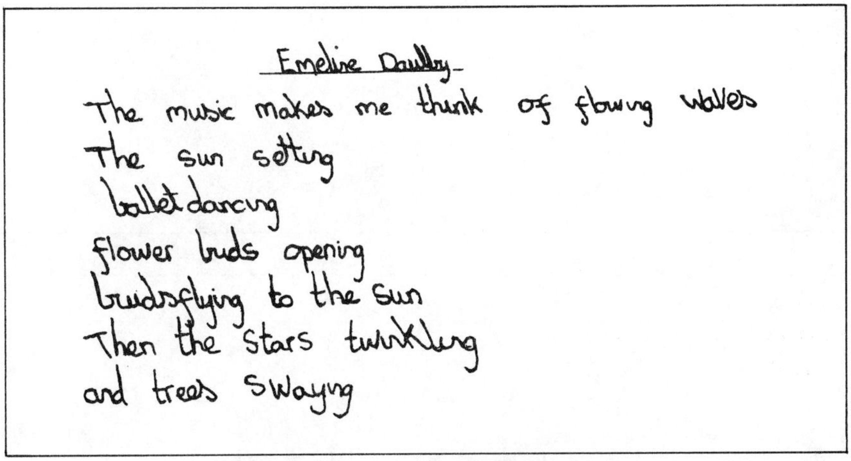

Roses opening
A hang glider
A stream flowing down a mountainside
The sun setting into the sea
A ballerina in a spotlight
A glider
Birds flying
Gentle waves lapping on the shore
A yacht on a calm sea
A violinist
Old fashioned ladies in crinolines
A moon and stars

Emeline Daulby

The music makes me think of flowing waves
The sun setting
ballet dancing
flower buds opening
buds flying to the sun
Then the stars twinkling
and trees swaying

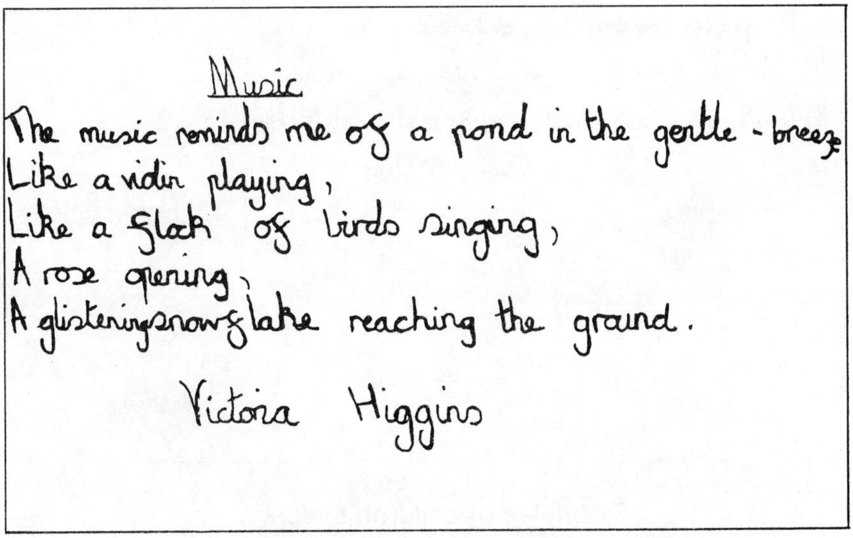

Music

The music reminds me of a pond in the gentle-breeze
Like a violin playing,
Like a flock of birds singing,
A rose opening,
A glistening snowflake reaching the ground.

Victoria Higgins

Examples of children's work

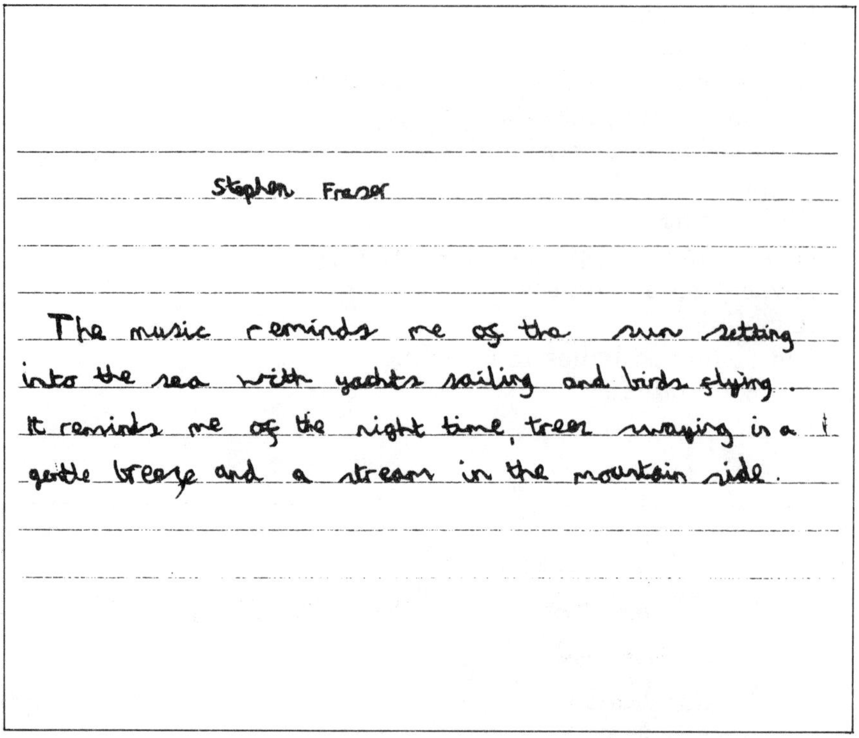

Stephen Fraser

The music reminds me of the sun setting into the sea with yachts sailing and birds flying. It reminds me of the night time, trees swaying in a gentle breeze and a stream in the mountain side.

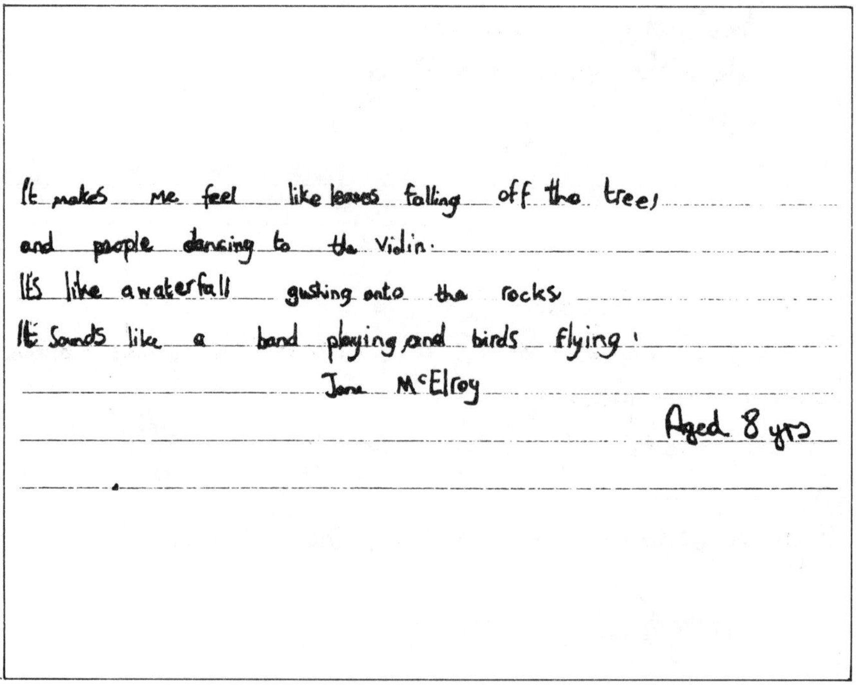

It makes me feel like leaves falling off the trees and people dancing to the violin.
It's like a waterfall gushing onto the rocks
It sounds like a band playing and birds flying.
Jane McElroy

Aged 8 yrs

Examples of children's work

Philip Unwin

The music makes me think of a sun-set in the forest and a river flowing gently. The blossom falling gently in the river or on land and a bird flying from tree to tree. The animals coming out like badger, deer, rabbit, black birds, a wood pecker, king-fisher, and a stork.

aged 8 yrs

The music makes me think of birds flying when the Sun sets down under the clouds. The wind pushes the Sea forward.

by
Jenny Nelson

Examples of children's work

Written and spoken detailed description of instruments

During a workshop session when the class could choose from a variety of activities allied to music, Paul (age 10) studied the snare drum and wrote the following detailed description of the drum, even including the height of the stand, the circumference of the skin and the number of screws.

'I like playing the snare drum. It is a special drum with a special sound. It fits on to a metal stand with three pieces to hold it properly. The drum is twelve inches in circumference. It is brown and has a white plasticy looking top. It has screws to tune it with. You can make the top tighter or looser. If it is tight it makes a higher sound when it is hit. If it is loose it makes a deeper sound because there is more to vibrate when you hit it. The thing that makes it sound different is a snare or trap made out of metal that you can fit against the bottom part of the skin like a trap or snare. That is why it is called the snare drum. When the snare is on it makes a metally sound when you hit it, a bit like maracas. It sounds like an army drum. You can play it with sticks or brushes. I like playing it very much.'

When we saw how much this normally reticent child had written we tried the idea out on other children. We received some very accurate descriptions of the instruments providing a context with which to link this music with mathematics.

Sounds around us

Tape recorders can be used to record a sequence of everyday sounds for children to identify, and talk or write about. One successful tape had the following sequence of early morning sounds.

Alarm clock bell
Bed creaking
Footsteps across the floor
Tap running in the bathroom
Lavatory flushing
Electric shaver
Footsteps down the stairs
Crockery clattering
Kettle boiling

Kettle whistling
Toaster popping
Newspaper falling on mat
Milkman rattling bottles
Doors opening and closing
Cat miaowing for food
Crockery noises
Letters falling from the letterbox to the floor.

After the tape had been played, the children had a lively discussion as to what the sounds were and how they differed from early morning sounds in their own homes. They were recalling sounds they had heard and differentiating between them. They discussed whether they were high or low, loud or quiet, etc.

Teaching aids

You can provide teaching aids for music as for any other subject. Workcards in the music area give the child the opportunity to work alone. These cards can be graded according to the children's ability. This means that a child can go to the music area unsupervised and carry out a music-related activity without teacher supervision. This increases the child's confidence in her/his ability to make music, and places music within the framework of classroom activity instead of making it a subject to be undertaken separately and always under a teacher's direction. The cards can relate to any musical activity, for example

1 Play a tune on the middle five notes of the xylophone.
2 Play this rhythm on the tambourine

   | ⊓ | |
  taa tate taa taa

3 Make and write down a rhythm of your own.
4 Find a partner. Choose an instrument each. Using the instruments, have a conversation which is:
   happy
   sad
   angry.
5 Find the highest note on the glockenspiel.
6 Which instruments can you play a tune on? Write down their names.

For younger children it is a good idea to have cards labelling the instruments. These can be used by the teacher with a group of children in a recognition game. Holding up a card with tambourine written on it, the teacher can say 'Paul, bring me this instrument.' Older children can carry out more complicated tasks which again help to give confidence and develop ability in the purposeful handling of instruments. One such task might be to compose a short piece for one of the following titles:

> Winter
> The sea
> A windy day
> Moonlight

Again the advantage is that children can use the musical instruments available without supervision and see musical instruments as a necessary part of the classroom equipment.

Further extensions of vocabulary

The children can make their own vocabulary books of words relating to music. They can make books describing musical experiences. One class of 7-year-olds went to sing at a non-competitive music festival and made a class book about their outing. The coach was as exciting to them as the singing but the event was important enough to make a book which was displayed in the classroom.

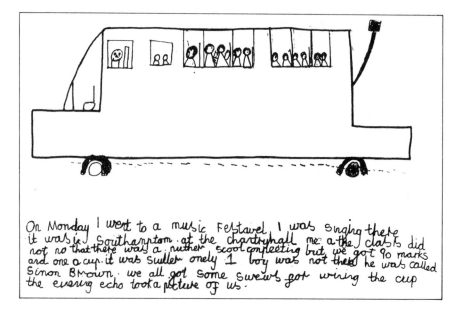

on monday the 10th of may we went to southampton
to the chantry hall for a ve Music festiffil. we wone a
cup and got 90 marks and got a certificate aswell. we sang
the lord of the dance and five little sneckled frogs.
I new we would win the cup. I also got some opal fruits

The music festival

Children can make books about their favourite instrument or piece of music. You can make a list of tapes or records you have listened to and display it in the hall. Many schools have a CD or tape of the week for the children to listen to as they come into assembly. This can be shown with the composer's name and perhaps a picture of the composer or the sleeve of the record. You can encourage the children to bring in to school any items or photographs relating to music from newspapers or magazines. You can display posters advertising musical events in the local community. In one school the children ran a weekly radio news programme using the schools inter-communication system and an item of musical news was always collected and read by the children. If any child had passed a music exam or acquired a new instrument or tape or record, or taken part in, or been to see any musical event, this was considered newsworthy. If they had learnt a song they particularly enjoyed or composed a song or piece of music they were particularly pleased with, this was also included. You can ensure that there are reference books and music books available in the school library or on general bookshelves. There is now a wide selection of reference books suitable for primary school children and their teachers. There are also books with a musical theme, (see pages 110–114).

Young children enjoy looking at song books, finding a song they know and reading the song as they sing it, sometimes pointing to the notes as they sing them. This, together with writing their own scores, reinforces the concept of a symbol representing a sound and the recognition of sounds and pauses or silences. They realise very quickly that the written notes match the movement of their voices. With older children this is another opportunity to explain how to use the notation. There are now excellent video tapes, films and TV programmes to help the teacher and children to enlarge their experience of music. These provide models for children to draw upon in using musical instruments and the voice in both spontaneous and structured activities of their own. In pursuing such creative activities the child is developing intuition, reasoning, creativity, memorisation and judgement. Teaching aids have their place and often provide good starting points but cannot take the place of practical experience.

Stimulus for composition

We can sometimes find a piece of writing which stimulates the children to musical composition. A class of 6-year-olds was listening to 'The Iron Man' by Ted Hughes read to them by their teacher. The story provoked an immediate response and they made a large iron man to display in the classroom. A large collection of metal objects, such as nails, scissors, graters, potato peelers, sieves, egg slicers, saucepan lids were brought in from home for him to eat. Adrian hit two nails together and said 'We could make some music for him with these.'

Linzi   *'Could we make some music for the Iron Man?'*
Teacher   *'What will the music be like?'*
Adrian   *'Loud and clattery'*
James   *'Hard and banging'*

After a great deal of discussion the following piece was composed and this score is what the children drew to help them to play their sounds at an assembly. One of the class pointed to the symbols while they were being played.

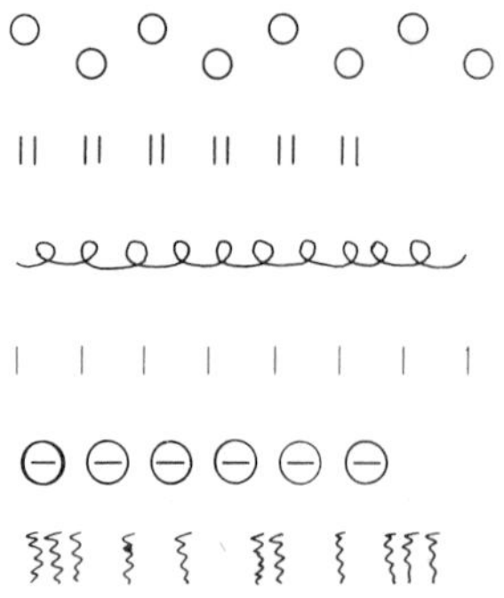

1	○ ○ ○ ○ ○ ○ ○ ○	napkin rings of different sizes
2	‖ ‖ ‖ ‖ ‖ ‖	spoons hit together
3	ℓℓℓℓℓℓℓℓℓℓ	battery rattling in a tin can
4	| | | | | | | |	nails suspended and hit
5	⊖ ⊖ ⊖ ⊖ ⊖ ⊖	pan lid hit with metal beater
6	⅗⅗ ⅗ ⅗ ⅗⅗ ⅗ ⅗⅗⅗	various graters rubbed with spoons

The children discovered through experimentation that most objects sounded better when suspended and so they threaded string through saucepan lids and wrapped cotton round nails, etc. This led to a discussion on vibration.

Kettle chant

Children soon regard anything and everything as possible instruments with which to enhance narratives of all kinds. Similarly the sounds made by an everyday object can provide the stimulus for a piece of written music. The name of an object can be broken into syllables and made into a chant. The sounds made can be used as a sound sequence. A group of 8-year-olds in the school kitchen listened to the jug kettle and came back to their teacher with an idea.

Lucy   'We could do a piece about the kettle sounds'
Teacher   'In what way?'
Lucy   'We could start from when you fill it and listen to the sounds'

The following piece was produced:

1 Pour water in
2 Plug in
3 Switch on
4 Hum
5 Water boils, gets louder
6 Steam out of spout as water boils
7 Kettle switches off
8 Unplug

Sound sequence

Kettle Chant

Fill the kettle
Boil the kettle
Faster than a pan

Boil the kettle
Pour the water
Drink it when you can

We clapped the rhythm of the chant and practised saying the words loudly and quietly. We played the rhythm on percussion instruments without saying the words aloud but thinking them. We played the chant as slowly as we could and then as quickly. The children had to watch the conductor carefully and chant together, again emphasising the importance of starting from silence. We thought of brand names of tea and made them into a rhythmic chant.

    ⊓   ⊓   ⊓   ⊓⊓

Ty phoo   Quick Brew   Tet leys   P G Tips

These exercises were fun to do and as the ideas came from the children they entered into them wholeheartedly.

Another class of 8/9-year-olds composed their own sound stories, working in pairs with one child writing the story and the other writing her/his own score and playing the sound effects. Children searched the school and playground for the right material to produce the most realistic sound. They were very critical of each others ideas and some strong disagreements took place. In all of this communication, a great deal of discussion of the sound properties of their finds took place.

Joanne   *'That waste bin doesn't make a deep enough noise for a monster's footsteps'*

Simon   *'It's not a very large monster'*

Joanne   *'No, but it's got to be frightening'*

During our conversations with young children we encouraged awareness of sounds in the environment in any given situation. Mary (age 5) was describing the high wind of the previous night.

Mary   *'It whistled and blew like this Whoo'* (rushing around the room)

Teacher   *'Was it the same all the time?'*

Mary   *'No it went quiet and then it was loud and then quiet again'*

Shilpi   *'I didn't like it, the rain hit our windows with a crash'*

Teacher   *'Was the rain making a hard sound or a soft sound?'*

Shilpi   *'Very hard, I thought the window was breaking up'*

Peter   *'The wind was rushing around and around like this! whoosh-!'* (rushing around the room)

The teacher took advantage of their interest to ask for words and phrases for a sound poem and suggestions for instruments to accompany it.

Blowing hard (*voices*)
Rushing around the house (*drums fast taps*)
Whistling loudly
Quiet at first getting louder (*newspapers flapped*)
Rain like pebbles on the window (*maracas*)
Rain lashing the air (*cymbals scraped*)
Dustbin lids clattering along the path (*cymbal hit*)
Leaves rustling (*newspaper*)
Wind whipping the trees
The actual storm (*all or some of the sounds can be played as the children feel appropriate*)

This poem was taped for the children to listen to and appraise.

You can encourage the children to write about their own musical experiences, the lives of composers and about instruments they enjoy playing. Simon (age 8) said he liked the violin because he liked the sound of its name. Class books can be made about a trip to a concert or music festival, or about a concert in the school by visiting musicians. Children can describe their reactions to a particular piece of music.

A class of 11-year-olds worked together to produce a poem about a haunted house.

Ghosts howling and crying like banshees (*voices*)
Monsters' heavy footsteps (*slow bass drum*)
A coffin lid slams down (*tambour*)
Bats squeaking (*recorder tops*)
Skeletons join in a ghostly dance (*wooden sticks on the xylophone*)
Owls hoot (*voice*)
A door creaks open (*guiro*)
Blood drips from the ceiling (*taps on a tambourine*)
Rats scurry across the floor (*maracas*)
Chains rattling (*chains*)
Low moaning is heard (*voices*)
An organ plays (*low notes on piano with loud pedal on*)

Several ideas, both words and sounds were discussed and rejected. The whole class became involved and became very interested in obtaining the most suitable sounds.

Sound is the raw material of communication and of music. We aim to encourage children to be aware of the sounds around them, to discriminate between them, to be aware of all kinds of music and sounds as an important part of their environment. This awareness should give enjoyment and stimulation to experiment with sounds in relation to language.

4 Scoring

We have seen how to give children the means to begin to learn the language of music, to experiment with sound-producing materials around them and to listen to, and form some opinions of all kinds of music. We also need to encourage children to record their own compositions in order to be able to play them again and also to show some progression and development. This essential part of music making can be achieved without the help of a specialist musician. An enthusiastic and sensitive approach is more important than expert knowledge which may even inhibit the flow of composition. When the music becomes more mature and complicated, then some knowledge of form is essential but a lack of this knowledge should not inhibit the non-specialist teacher from giving children the opportunity to order their sound patterns in some way into melodic, harmonic and rhythmic patterns. These will not always follow conventional lines but young children are not inhibited by the need to conform. One teacher with a class of 6-year-olds encouraged them to write simple melodies. When the tunes were presented to her, she went to some trouble to write them out on the treble stave working them into conventional time signatures and **C F** and **G** key signatures and making a book of 'Our Class Tunes'. When she played the 'real music' back to her class she realised how much of the originality and excitement had been lost through her intervention.

Getting started

There are several starting points for scoring composition. One way of introducing and devising an informal way of notation is to select three or four small unpitched percussion instruments and to give each child in the class or group, paper and the relevant number of coloured pencils or crayons. You can then play a sound on one instrument, for example a drum, and ask the children to choose a colour and draw the sound. Something like the following will result:

○   ○   ○   ○   ○   ○

If you make the sound start quietly and grow louder you may get:

○   ○   ○   ○   ○   ◯

You can then play a different instrument, perhaps the maracas with a continuous sound. The children choose another colour and draw this sound, which perhaps might be:

〜〜〜〜〜〜〜〜〜〜〜〜〜〜〜〜〜〜

You can then choose an instrument with a long sound dying away, for example an Indian bell, and the children again change their colour and draw the sound. The following are two examples of children's work:

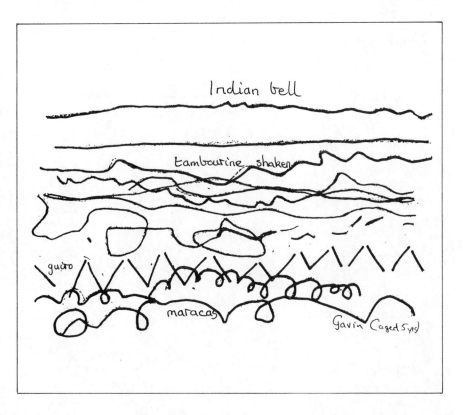

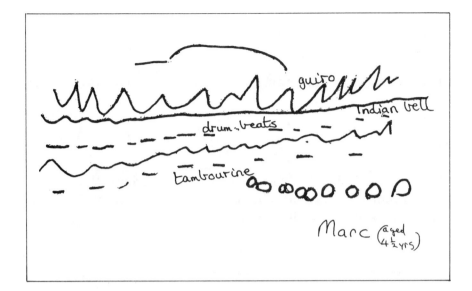

You can ask the young children to keep the drawing secret so that copying is not encouraged but it is surprising how the symbols written by children are very similar. You can then decide which symbols to adopt for the scores. The following were decided upon by a class of 7-year-olds.

short sound	——
long sound	———————————
sound going higher	⟋
sound going lower	⟍
loud sound getting quieter	◯ ◯ ◯ ○
continuous sound	∿∿∿
continuous up and down	⋀⋀⋀⋀

interrupted sound	— — — — — —
fast continuous	(fast continuous wavy line)
fast interrupted	- - - - - - - - - - - - - -
slow continuous	(slow continuous wavy line)
slow interrupted	— — — — —
slow dying away	(curved line dying away)

We became very conscious of the silence between sounds and how important it was. We discussed the type of sound produced. Was it short or long, smooth or jerky, high or low, and we debated the best type of symbols to use. We were devising a shorthand of sound. The children were learning that symbols on a paper could represent sounds, and that those symbols could be read and translated into music. The idea of left to right visual representation of sound was also being reinforced. Every child in the class was very involved and if any work resulted in a sound pattern which they could translate into sound, they felt they had really achieved something of their own. They had to decide how many times they were going to play each instrument and then they wrote this on our score. Eventually they split into groups and the following is some of the work produced and written about. Some of the children wished to incorporate instruments such as chime bars and the glockenspiels.

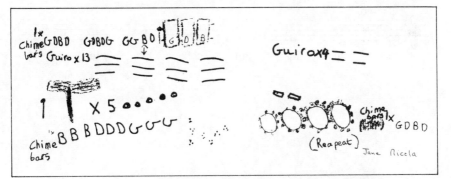

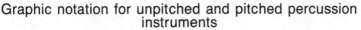

Graphic notation for unpitched and pitched percussion instruments

Using pitched instruments

The use of pitched instruments leads us on to another stage of composing tunes. Most of the pitched instruments in schools have the name of the note written on them. The chime bars, xylophone and glockenspiel are marked with the letters of the notes. At least middle **C** of the piano can also be marked if required.

The names of the notes in the lines and spaces of the treble clef can be taught and if necessary learnt by the teacher.

The traditional way to remember this is Every Good Boy Deserves Favour (**EGBDF**) and that the spaces spell **FACE** but children will devise their own sayings if asked. We thought of

Elephants Get Big Dirty Feet

Every Green Bus Drives Fast

Each Girl Bought Dressy Frocks

and these helped us to remember.

We can teach the names of a scale in sol-fa.

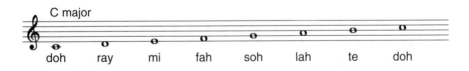

In the song from the 'Sound of Music', 'Doh a deer' is one way of reinforcing this idea. The feeling for cadence or going home to 'doh' is something that can come through experience. Alan (age 6) was using three chime bars **B D A** to compose a short tune that was obviously in the key of **G**, i.e. **G** was 'doh' and he was dancing around the room saying 'I can't make it finish'. When he found a **G** chime bar he successfully finished his tune.

Children who are learning the recorder, even when they have only learnt the first three notes **B A G**, will often compose short tunes if encouraged. Robert (age 7) brought in a book of tunes that he had written when he was practising his recorder. His efforts inspired other children in the class to do the same.

Composing for a theme

Compositions do not always need to be written down. If a teacher is not happy to progress to more formal scoring it is always possible to use the tape recorder. Simple rules of the form of music can often be learnt with the children.

Another starting point may be a piece of music you have listened to which tells a story (known as programme music) for example

The Sorcerer's Apprentice Dukas
The Thieving Magpie Rossini
Fingal's Cave Mendelssohn
Night on the Bare Mountain Musorgsky
The Firebird Stravinsky

These are examples of music where the composer has explored sound to convey a special meaning. Children can be encouraged to do the same and create music on a theme.

On the following pages are some compositions and descriptions of the composing process by 8-year-olds. All the examples relate to winter.

○○○ three Drums
~~five~~ + triangle
XXXX four chimebar ~~====~~ guiro three
○○○○○○○ seven Drums | Winter by
~~#~~ three triangles ~~======~~ | Kristel Sophie Jonathan
~~XXXXXXXX~~ eight chimebars | guiro Six
~~######~~ r nine triangle

∞ two Drum
\# two traingle
\#\# two chimebarG B ₧together
~~######~~ guiro two
~~+++++XXX~~ guiro ten
ten traingle ₧together.

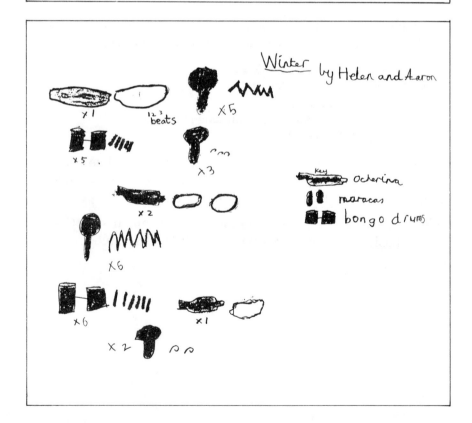

Winter by Helen and Aaron

x1 123 beats x5
x5 x3
x2 Key Ocherina
x6 maracas
x6 x1 bongo drums
x2

Jenny Kiggins | I played winter music on a bottle cymbals and two chime bars. I made a sound patten and wrote it down

I composed music for winter. I blew across a bottle and shook the bells and hit four chime bars. They made a lovely tune. It took a long time to think out.

Cheryl

We chose maracas, bongo drums and ocherlra because they sounded wintry. We made a key up to tell people what our Instuments were. We wrote them down.

by Aaron and Helen

The children can take turns in playing to each other and asking for constructive criticism. Decisions have to be made and adhered to. When listening to one composition for a story about the sea the discussion became quite heated.

Gary   *'Why does the cymbal sound so loud? We can't hear the drum.'*

Christina   *'Those are the waves crashing onto the shore. The drum is the sea but the wave crash drowns out its sound every now and again.'*

Gary   *'Then you should have the drum softer at first and the cymbal coming in loudly at a definite time just like the sea really does.'*

Mary   *'What is that high recorder sound?'*

Christina   *'Those are seagulls.'*

Gary   *'I've never heard seagulls during a storm.'*

The tape recorder is very useful during these sessions. You can hear the different timbres of the instruments used. You can hear the balance of one group of instruments against another. You can decide whether the speed or tempo at which you are playing is right. You may decide when listening to improvised compositions that the individual instruments are swamped and it all sounds like a muddle. Then you can go back and re-structure to clarify and make the piece more musical. Perhaps a solo instrument can be played with the others joining in or ceasing to play at a given moment. Perhaps the dynamics: loudness and quietness of different parts can be changed. You may decide to repeat one part or maybe cut out another part altogether. All the time you are listening, appraising and deciding what will be the final piece to perform.

Young children composing tunes often swoop from one end of an instrument to another and so we can restrict them by giving them three or five notes to compose their tune on. These tunes are easier for them to remember and repeat. You can 'doctor' instruments such as glockenspiels and xylophones in order to restrict the range. This is especially useful if you are composing a song as it is useful to have a tune that can be sung. Also, if you are to compose a simple harmony, it is easier to begin with the notes of a chord. These are not hard and fast rules and there are always exceptions. The non-specialist teacher will find it easier to have a couple of chord changes for accompaniment. You can compose a class song by putting words together first, thinking of the rhythm of the first line, having your five chime bars ready and asking for a volunteer to play the first line. Once you have begun you can ask for similar help to compose further. You can decide which phrases you are going to use and how to put them together. You may decide to have a very simple repeated melody, to have another melody in the middle and go back to the first melody to finish. Are you going to have verses and a chorus or not?

A class of 6/7-year-olds were studying owls and could not find a suitable song for their assembly where they were telling the rest of the school about their work.

Samantha *'Why don't we compose our own?'*
Nicholas *'Tu whit tu whoo'*
James   *'Tu whit tu whoo I wish I knew'*

The words came first and then we composed a tune. This is the result and we wrote it out with the names of the notes underneath and sang it unaccompanied.

The Owl Song

Tu whit tu whoo
I wish I knew
I wish I knew what owls can do
They fly around
Without a sound
Then with a shriek they swoop right down
They catch the mice
Do they taste nice?
Tu whit tu whoo
I wish I knew
All through the night
With smoothest flight
Until the dawn
And then they're gone
Tu whit tu whoo
I wish I knew
I wish I knew what owls can do

The more singing children have done, the happier they will be during this kind of composition. If their ideas for songs have been taken seriously and if the criticism they have received has always been constructive then they will be able to volunteer a phrase or line without fear of rebuffal. Even if their suggestion is not used their confidence will not be destroyed if they are given a reason for the refusal and encouraged to try again. The way that the teacher intervenes is all important. It is the children's song with help from the teacher and not the other way round. Children who compose in this way learn their song very quickly and remember it for a long time because it is theirs. Again the tape recorder is very useful both as a record and for appraisal.

You can teach some simple musical terms for incorporating in the scores. Children enjoy the sound of the Italian words and practise saying them enthusiastically.

pianissimo (written pp)	very quiet
piano (written p)	quiet
forte (written f)	loud
fortissimo (written ff)	very loud

You can also use the repeat sign :‖. You can encourage the children to use the pentatonic scale or five note scale (the doh ray mi soh lah doh notes of the diatonic scale). The intervals between the notes make it possible for the notes to harmonise or sound pleasant when played together. We all hear children playing Chopsticks on the black notes of the piano and this works on the pentatonic principle. You can 'doctor' glockenspiels and xylophones so that the notes

     C D F G A
or **C D E G A**
or **D B F A B**
or **G A B D E**

are left for the children to compose with. This will result in some very pleasing sounds.

The purposes of composing are:

1 for its own sake because children enjoy the sounds they make;
2 to accompany words written by themselves either alone or in a group;
3 to fit a theme: the sea, power, ghosts, space etc.

If you accept the children's own way of writing their songs or tunes down, eventually they may progress to wishing to write their own tunes on manuscript paper. For this you can teach the note names of the treble stave. Then you come to the problem of writing rhythmically. Children may write their notes all the same way. As they progress they can learn the names of the notes used to show the length or duration of sounds. You can make flashcards for these and for the names of notes and make a game of learning them.

Where the strongest accents occur language has its own natural rhythmic groups of two, three and four. You can say a well known phrase and listen for the strong beat.

You feel the accent on the first beat of each bar

| ⌣ | ⌣ | ⌣ |
Piping down the valleys wild

Sometimes the heavy accent is on the second word and we start on an upbeat.

⌣ | ⌣ | ⌣ | ⌣ |
I wandered lonely as a cloud

The kind of music children hear when they are given the opportunity to compose is of paramount importance. The way they decide to write it down for future reference is important too but their music making in the early days should not be inhibited by worries about scoring. The aim is to give children the opportunity to compose and to record their compositions in some meaningful manner whether that be formal or not. Teachers who do not feel able to study musical form can still compose with their pupils.

Compositions

In one school four 10-year-old girls in year 6 composed a carol. They wrote the words first and then the melody using a glockenspiel and the piano. They then used Rhapsody software to put the carol onto the A3000 computer. Later they printed it out so that other children could sing it. They had all been learning the flute for a couple of years so they understood formal notation. Victoria worked out the harmony. That they had the confidence to attempt this and to achieve such an admirable result must in part be due to the attitude to music throughout the school, where most of the staff whether musical or not are involved under the guidance and enthusiasm of the teacher with responsibility for music. They also made a recording in a professional recording studio as a parent was involved in this professional field. One girl sang solo and the other three played keyboard and flute obligato accompaniment. The carol appears on pages 68−69.

A group of 5/6-year-olds worked on composition in their music corner using a keyboard, a glockenspiel, a triangle and a tambourine. Their music had structure, they were playing in turn and then together. The music was very loud and getting louder. Their class teacher suggested that they composed a lullaby for Teddy. She put the cot with Teddy near the music corner and this

A PERFECT CHRISTMAS

had the desired effect. The resulting composition was organised by the boy on the keyboard. He instructed the girl playing the triangle not to play all the time as it was too noisy and asked the girl on the glockenspiel to write her sequence of notes down on a piece of paper so that she remembered them. When asked if he should write his music down he replied that he could remember it as it was exactly what he had played the day before. This was confirmed by the other children. He did include his notes in the large score that was written by the children in case he wanted to play it again after the summer holidays.

Composing a lullaby for Teddy

You can sing or speak in two parts making one part an ostinato or persistent rhythmic accompaniment. These rhythmic patterns can be derived from rhythm games or poetry as well as songs, for example

Hush little baby

Mocking bird mocking bird

Many song books give examples of ostinato based accompaniments.

You can say poems or chants, for example

Gravy and potatoes in a big brown pot
Put them in the oven and serve them hot

serve them hot serve them hot   (ostinato)

You can say well known rhymes putting the stress on different words

Rain rain go away

Rain rain go away

Rain rain go away

With older children you can each take a book or a newspaper, choose a paragraph and read it over and over again following a conductor's signals (previously decided) to read

1 quietly, loudly
2 slowly, fast
3 loud getting quieter
4 quiet becoming loud
5 with a high pitched voice
6 with a low pitched voice
7 mixture of the two etc

You can tape the results and listen to the sound effect.

You can choose any short poem to accompany either a group of voices or instruments.

Doctor Foster went to Gloucester
In a shower of rain
He stepped in a puddle
Right up to his middle
And never went there again

Accompaniment

Pitter patter   Pitter patter
Pitter patter   Pitter patter

By the time children have reached key stage 2 they should be composing and recording their own compositions in some way. The method of recording they choose should be relevant to their experience. Their compositions should not be inhibited by the imposition of the formal kind of notation which has become acceptable to us over the years. There is a place for teaching this if it can be done at the same time as encouraging the children's own scoring. If you look at the scores produced by many modern composers you will see that staff notation is itself changing to accommodate modern music.

5 Science and sound

You can build on a child's natural curiosity and readiness to explore during music making to teach the child about sound. At primary school level this will not go too deeply into what is a very complex scientific subject but a surprising amount can be learnt by children aged up to 11. You will want to explore how we hear, make and send sounds.

Vibration

We can begin with some simple experiments on vibration. Vibration is a movement produced by hitting, shaking, plucking or blowing an object. This movement makes the object vibrate or shake and in turn the vibration produces a sound which makes the particles of air near it move, and in turn the next particles move and so on, producing a sound wave which travels outwards through some thick and some thin particles of air until the ear picks up the sound. If the vibrations are slow we hear a low note. If they are fast we hear a high note.

The auditory nerve can cut out expected sounds but not unexpected ones like the dripping of a tap in the night. We are able to tune in to sounds even when asleep like a mother who hears her baby's cry, as well as being able to cut out traffic or constant radio noise. The brain interprets sound and has an active response to known signals even when we do not actively listen. You can demonstrate this to children by asking them to be quiet and to listen to 'silence'. The children quickly become aware of sounds they were not aware of when not actively listening. The earlier this training is begun the better, and very young children enjoy listening to see what they can hear. Here is a list of sounds heard by a class of 4/5-year-olds.

A bird singing on a tree in the playground
Traffic on the nearby road
The teacher's voice in the class next to ours

An aeroplane
A bluebottle on the window
The milk float on the road outside
A police siren

There are many simple activities to investigate the pitch of sound. You can hold a ruler on a table and hit the free end and watch it vibrate. You can vary the pitch of the note produced by varying the length of ruler left free to vibrate. A longer ruler produces a lower note.

Guitar, twanging ruler and recorder

You can twang rubber bands stretched across boxes or stretched from your teeth (if you are careful not to hit yourself in the face). The sounds produced depend upon the initial thickness of the band and the amount of tension placed on it but you should find that the thicker bands vibrate more slowly and produce a sound lower in pitch than the thinner ones. You can suspend plant pots or nails or spoons of different sizes and hit them. The sound produced will vary in pitch according to the size of the object vibrating.

Emeline Oaulby aged 9 yrs

How to make a box guitar

To make a box guitar you will need a box and for elastic bands and then put the elastic bands (for) on the box and then you can play your box guitar
thiker elastic bands make lower sonds
thiner elastic bands make higher sounds.

You can discover that the material of the objects hit and those you hit with, can make the sound change. You can teach the older children that the number of times the object vibrates per second is known as the frequency. High frequency produces a high pitched sound and low frequency a low pitched sound. An electric food mixer demonstrates that as the speed of the beaters increases so the sound becomes higher.

You can blow across the top of a bottle and make a sound. You can vary the pitch of the sound produced by putting water in the bottle. The note produced is higher the more water there is in the bottle (i.e. the less air there is to vibrate). If you tap the bottle when it's full, half-full and empty you will discover that the sound varies again with the amount of water. This time the bottle with less water in it will make a lower sound when hit because you are hitting the bottle to make the glass vibrate and not blowing the air inside it.

We played stretched rubber-band and them.

1. The thinner we pulled them the higher the note went.
2 The thick bands made a low note
The thick bands vibrate slowly
The thin bands vibrate quickly

We did an experiment with rulers
The more ruler we left over the desk to twang the lower the note. Adrian aged 7yrs

Description of experiments

Vibration making rice jump around on a cymbal

Musical instruments and vibration

If you hold a piece of grass between your fingers and blow, you can produce a note. You can relate these experiments to wind instruments such as the clarinet, bassoon and oboe where double and single reeds are used to produce a sound. When playing the flute you blow across the edge of the hole much as you do across a bottle. Brass instruments work on the principle of the player using her/his breath to vibrate the lips against the end of a pipe, making the air column in the tube vibrate. Different methods of vibration make different notes. The simpler brass instruments work with a fixed tube length. The more complicated instruments have valves to open up lengths of pipe. The trombone has a slide to vary the length of tube which varies the note. You can demonstrate timbre on these instruments by playing the same note on as many pitched instruments as are available and drawing the children's attention to the same note but the differing sounds produced. You can look at string instruments such as violin, cello, double bass, harp, guitar and realise that the sound is changed by using pegs to tighten or loosen different thicknesses of strings, and by vibrating the strings by plucking them with the fingers or scraping them with a bow. An electric guitar player can make notes last longer by using special effects such as a reverb box. Musicians control the way that sounds are produced using many different techniques.

You can make your own string instrument by fixing a broom handle into a cardboard box and attaching a length of cord to the top of the handle and stretching it down to the box. You can then strum the cord varying the note by varying the tension on the cord with your other hand.

You can demonstrate the effect of vibration in percussion instruments by playing the different sizes of for example drums, cymbals or triangles and even the youngest child will realise that the small drum produces a higher sound than the larger drum, and the small cymbal a higher note than the larger one. They can hear that even by tightening the tambourine or drum with their thumb, the note varies. They can 'stop' cymbals, chime bars, triangles and Indian bells by touching them and stopping the vibration. If you put rice or sand on the top of a cymbal or tambourine and hit it you can watch the rice moving around with the vibration. You can vary the attack to see what effect it has on the sound produced. If you hit hard, a louder sound results, and with a cymbal or Indian bell you produce a longer lasting sound.

The children in a class of 8-year-olds decided to make a graph of the duration of sounds they produced by measuring them with a stop watch. They realised that the effect depended on how hard they hit but they listened carefully and came to some interesting conclusions. The cymbal made the sound of longest duration followed closely by the Indian bell. The shaken tambourine produced a sound of very short duration however hard it was shaken. This is the result of their experiment.

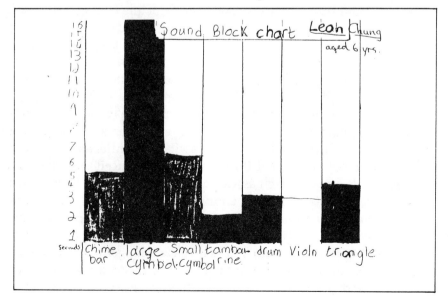

Duration of sound

You can also demonstrate that sound waves can be seen when a tuning fork is hit and suspended in a bowl of water. Waves can be seen coming from the fork. If you can borrow an oscillosope, you can watch the characteristics of sounds being reproduced on the screen. We discovered with a class of 7-year-olds that the high pitched sounds appeared to have a smaller wavelength than the low pitched sounds. This tied in very well with the work we had been doing with sound patterns.

All these facts can be demonstrated using real and home-made instruments. Lucy (age 10) brought in her clarinet and demonstrated it to the rest of the class. A parent who played in a jazz group brought in a guitarist, a drummer with full kit, his own marimba and a double bass player. When he asked what they should play to the children I asked for jazz but also requested that each instrumentalist would explain how her/his instrument worked in order to get the children to ask questions about the instruments. Under careful supervision, the children were also allowed to play the instruments. It was a very successful afternoon. The husband of the school cleaning lady is a drummer in his spare time and he brought in his drum kit and corrected some of our percussion techniques. There is nothing to replace watching the real thing and hearing live music.

The voice

The voice is capable of an endless variety of sounds: shouting, laughing, singing, speaking quietly or loudly, using different voices or different accents. The voice can be used to demonstrate dynamics, timbre, duration, speed and rhythm. How do we all do it? It begins with our taking a breath. If we run out of breath, we run out of voice. The breath passes over our vocal chords which vibrate to make a sound. These chords are pieces of skin in the windpipe in a box of cartilage situated in the neck called the voice box or larynx. You can feel the larynx as your Adam's apple. The brain arranges that your chords are stretched to just the right amount so that when the breath passes over them, they make the sound you require. By placing a finger lightly on the larynx you can feel the vibration. Tightly stretched chords produce faster vibrations and so higher pitched sounds. Loosely stretched chords vibrate more slowly and make lower pitched sounds. Quiet or loud sounds are made by controlling the amount of air breathed out. You make loud sounds by expelling a lot of air and quiet sounds by using less air. Cavities in the forehead, nose and cheek bones modify and vary the sounds made. Tongues, teeth and jaws do not vibrate but are used to alter the sounds of the vibrating air passing through them.

Feeling the vibration of the larynx

Every voice is unique and the children will appreciate this by listening to the voices around them and hearing the differences. You can tape people singing and speaking and see if you can identify members of the class or staff by their voices.

Sounds in the modern world

Sounds are sent in our modern world in a variety of ways, mostly electronic. The children accept such marvels as telephones, radios and televisions as normal. You can ask the children how they thought sounds were transmitted before these modern machines. You can tell them about the talking drums of Africa, the smoke signals of the American Indians. You can show how hunters and cowboys would put their ears to the ground and hear the vibration of herds of buffalo and other animals moving towards them. The children can crouch close to the ground to discover what they can hear. They can devise ways of making a megaphone. They can see how the sound is amplified by choosing different shapes and materials and decide which has the best effect. They can listen to heating pipes which pass from one room to another to see if they can hear anything from the next room. You can make string telephones by threading a length of string to the bottom of yoghurt cartons or cans. One child speaks into one carton whilst the other child listens to the carton at the other end of the string. You can experiment using different containers and strings to see if the sound varies.

You can measure levels of sound using a sound level meter and make children more aware of the noise in our environment. You can devise ways of measuring the levels of sound around you. Decide which is the noisiest part of the school, which noises are liked or disliked and whether the teachers dislike the same or different noises than the children. You can think about people who work in noisy environments, for example road builders using pneumatic drills, factory workers, people living near a busy motorway, people living near or working in airports. You can also discuss how sounds can benefit people. Wayne (age 6) said 'My dad honks his car horn to get people out of the way'. Clare said 'It could be a fire engine telling us the fire is going to be put out'. Joseph said 'We have a smoke alarm in our house'. David said 'You can make people happy if you make happy sounds or sad if you cry'. Noise pollution is a whole subject in itself and is very relevant to today's children whose hearing can be damaged by listening to loud 'pop' music.

You can experiment with different materials to see what makes the best insulator against loud sounds. What makes the best ear muffs — newspaper, cotton, polystyrene, plastic? You can discuss who has to wear them at work and why. You can see if you can hear a sound from a long way off as well as nearby. Can you really hear a pin drop? You can play a game to try to discover from which direction a sound is coming. You can discover if high and low sounds can be heard equally well. You can test your ears by covering each in turn to see if you hear equally well with each. You can discuss what it must be like to have impaired hearing and what can be done to help people with this disability. You can talk about the speed of sound, and if Concorde passes over the school as it does over some schools, you can explain that it is the only western supersonic plane in existence, it can fly faster than the speed of sound and the bang we hear is the plane accelerating through that sound barrier.

You might be able to examine the audiometer used by the school nurse when giving a hearing test. Most children will have experienced this and will happily sit with their earphones on listening carefully for the beep produced usually in each ear alternately, and clapping or giving some signal when they can hear it. In the sweep audiometer test the sounds vary in intensity and vary from quite a loud sound to a fairly faint one. The children can watch the needle on the machine in operation and realise that sound can be measured, usually in decibels.

Sound is a fascinating topic and there are many starting points for working with children of all ages and levels. It is especially relevant to children today. You can encourage them to discriminate and evaluate the great variety of sounds around them. They can decide when to listen and what to switch off. If they understand how sound is produced and what a very important part it plays in so many ways in their lives perhaps they can learn to have a more discriminating attitude towards the sounds around them.

6 Cross-curricular music

Music is a vast subject with a large repertoire. It can be very difficult for the non-specialist to know where to start and what to choose to teach. Some schools decide upon a general theme to be taught throughout a year group on the whole school which links all creative work in each class for each term or half-term. These themes are usually broad-based and give us somewhere to start. Some of the most successful I have seen which have offered opportunities for music are:

Power	Europe
Water	Stones
Outer space	Holes
Flight	Colours
Animals	Magic

In one primary school power was chosen.

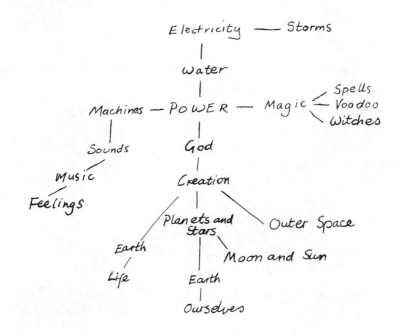

Each class took one aspect and the teachers chose powerful music to listen to, for example

> *Pomp and Circumstance* Elgar
> *Finlandia* Sibelius
> *War Requiem* Britten

We discussed why the music sounded so powerful and decided that it was the choice of instruments for example drums, trumpets. It was also due to the tempo it was played at and the feelings that the music inspired within us. Sibelius uses several string instruments playing together and the deep slow music made a powerful sound. Children soon learned to distinguish between the different families of instruments and to discuss their effect. The class noticed different timbres of the instruments used to create the required effect. Magic made the children think not only of witches and warlocks but also of voodoo and black magic. This inspired the creation of drum sequences and chants. We composed some African drum sequences and listened to tapes of African drum music.

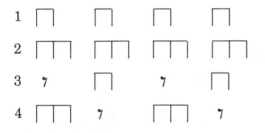

We wrote a poem about the power of electricity and chose percussion instruments to accompany it.

> Powerful but unseen (*bass drum: quiet getting louder*)
> Brings up light and warmth
> Illuminating our lives (*glockenspiel:* **E' C E'**)
> At the flick of a switch
> Drives trams and trains (*guiro*)
> Runs machines
> Frightens us in storms (*2 cymbals*)
> Generated by water (*tambour scratched*)
> Works the television
> Makes our lives easier

The children painted while listening to 'Mars' from The Planets by Gustav Holst. Mars is known as the 'Bringer of War' and is the first piece in the suite of seven pieces written in 1915 during the first world war. The children's paintings were in strong dark colours, menacing and powerful and this confirmed my experience that children often demonstrate the structure of music in their paintings.

Dance

It has already been mentioned how a single small percussion instrument can be used as a stimulus. In one school I visited a class of 7-year-olds who had been given the words:

Hop
Step
Jump
Wobble

then worked in groups taking turns to play the small percussion instruments they had chosen to demonstrate each word in turn.

Hop

Wobble

Children of all ages enjoy moving to a strong beat and they do not discriminate between pop and classical. They respond to the beat and the mood. This is very evident when young children come into assembly. Whilst the older children come sedately into the hall listening to the tape being played, the little ones dance in and move their hands in time to the music. Whilst working in a team teaching situation with a class of 6-year-olds the children were moving freely around the hall to 'Waltz in D' by Tchaikovsky. One child came over to me and described how he had been dancing.

*'I moved round and round over there by the door and did some
quick steps in the middle and moved my arms like a windmill
until I got to you.'*

He was very excited and knew exactly what he'd been doing and
I asked him if he could draw it. We brought some large pieces of
paper and crayons and asked the class to draw their dance patterns.
The results were very complex and detailed. Since then we have
incorporated this as part of a dance lesson either alone or in pairs
or groups. One teacher asked children to dance as though their feet
were dipped in paint and to be conscious of the pattern their feet
were making on the floor. This encouraged the children to use the
space provided and to move in every direction instead of going round
and round. With older children we discussed choreography.

We also used colour as a stimulus. When working on a theme of
light and dark we borrowed a spotlight and drew the curtains in
the hall to block the daylight. The children danced in the dark and
then moved into the spotlight. We found that the children moved
cautiously looking around to see what was in the shadows of the
dark area but they changed when they reached the spotlight into
freer and fearless movements. We listened to various pieces of music
to decide what was suitable for dancing in the light and dancing
in the dark. We decided on the music 'Night on a Bare Mountain'
by Musorgsky for the dark, and 'Firebird' by Stravinsky for the
light but these were personal choices and many other pieces of
music would have fitted. We also used coloured filters and noticed
the difference to the movement if red or green or blue were used.
We chose percussion instruments to dance to in these colours. Red
was always the drums and green and blue were triangles, Indian
bells and glockenspiels. Green and blue evoked soft, dreamy
movement whilst red and orange evoked strong, vigorous
movement. The children also danced on different textures of
material, hessian, nylon fur and large pieces of nylon. They danced
tentatively on the hessian and rolled around in the fur and dug
their feet into it. They threw the nylon up into the air, ran around
with it floating behind them, swirling it around in the air. Then
they were asked to describe how they felt when they were dancing,
perhaps writing a poem or saying what they felt into a tape
recorder. Here are some of the results:

Emma (age 7)
*The white nylon made me think of a seagull
Swooping across the blue sky
Lifting me up into white clouds
Then landing on a wave*

Jane (age 7)
I was the yellow sun
In the bright light
Gold all around me
I was warm and strong
I felt happy

Tom
I am a furry animal
Creeping on the floor
Small and cuddly
Soft to stroke

Maria (age 8)
I am red
Like the sun at night
Like the sky when the sun has gone
Like a dragon
I am burning up
I move faster and faster through the fire

We then talked about texture and how this applies to music. We listened to music of all kinds and related it to smooth, hard, soft, jagged etc.

Music from the past

Having seen how music can be related to art, drama, language, you can also point out the part music has played in the history of our country and other countries of the world. You can go back to the way man began to make music and how it has always been a part of life. One class of 9-year-olds decided to think about medieval music. They looked at pictures of the instruments used in that era and acquired a psaltery to look at and try to play. The children were interested to learn how long people had been playing the recorder. We found a song 'Philip My Sparrow' and two jigs to play on recorders. We also listened to music by Praetorius and tapes of medieval church music.

A class of 11-year-olds was studying ancient Egypt. They decided to compose some suitable music and write their own scores as they thought the Egyptians would have recorded them. These are the results:

Music from around the world

We thought about music from hot countries and music from cold countries comparing the music of Spain and Italy and that of England and Finland. We thought about national characteristics in music and discussed how we could tell one country's music from another. We learnt songs in simple French and Spanish. One group of schools when studying Europe each decided to study one country of the EC. The school I worked in chose Spain and as well as learning about the customs of the country they also studied the music. They listened to guitar music with castanets and maracas. They listened to Spanish folk music and collected dolls and pictures of Spanish dancers. They also learnt some simple songs in Spanish. They visited other schools and listened to the songs the children had learnt there. A concert of songs and music from European countries was given for parents and the local community to enjoy.

You can play children the music of the great Russian composers and play tapes of the wonderful harmonies of Russian church music. You can introduce children to choruses from Italian opera. You can play the music of the great Polish composer Chopin and of the Czech Composers Dvořák and Smetana. Each time you play music you can point out the nationality of the composer and the era in which he lived.

There is a wealth of home produced folk and classical music from composers such as Handel, Elgar, Holst and Britten. Children should not get the idea that composers are all dead. You can perhaps play a selection of both popular and classical music by modern composers, for example John Cage, Sir Peter Maxwell Davies, Penderecki, Stockhausen.

Children can be introduced to Jamaican and West Indian music, to the soul music rhythms of reggae and rap and to Indian music on sitars. You can use festivals and feasts as a starting point. There are excellent books and tapes available for this purpose (see pages 110–114).

Listening to music

If you expose children to this wealth of material then you also need to teach them to listen, to absorb and to make a critical evaluation. The children will not enjoy everything but you can generate discussion and evaluation, treating their opinions (if they are realistic) with respect. You can listen to any music they may wish to bring in to play for you with the same attention as you require of them. Music brought in by the children is often a bridge between music at home and at school. A meaningful discussion can take place as to what they like to listen to and what you think they ought to be listening to. Popular music and jazz has its place here. You can teach social history through music, through sea shanties, work songs and the songs of the music hall, the protest songs of the '60s and later and songs of the two great wars. You can tell the stories of programme music and get children to learn to listen to music and to regard it as a living part of work in the classroom. You can give them time to reflect both on what they hear and what they have composed and encourage them to discuss their findings with each other and with you.

Assemblies

Assemblies are often a focal point for music in primary schools. There is usually a tape played to accompany children for coming into and leaving the assembly. The music can set the mood for the assembly and the children should be encouraged to come in quietly and listen to the music and not treat the tape as something to chat against. The staff should also observe this rule. I have found it useful to play a tape of extracts from the same piece of music every morning for a week and to display the title and composer of the music, and also to give the children a short history of the composer with date of birth, country of origin etc. This way even very young children get to know the names of composers and their music. If a special assembly is planned then music which ties in with the theme being discussed can be played. Dance can also be a part of assembly. On another occasion we were celebrating an Indian festival and Naina who was having dancing lessons gave a display of classical Indian dance in full costume. If a piece of music has been composed or learnt then there is a chance for it to be performed for the staff and children during assembly.

Most primary schools have a hymn practice once a week and with the variety of hymn books available to schools you can choose suitable hymns for the topics of the terms and also sing hymns from other cultures. Again I believe that children should always understand what they are singing about and the words of hymns should always be explained.

I do not subscribe to the idea of having words put on overhead projectors or the use of hymn books for very young children. Children learn the words much more easily by practice and imitation. If they rely on charts and books in general they will never really know the words. As the children get older they may use hymn books for more complicated words and music.

Assembly can also be a time when children who are learning an instrument can play for the school and perhaps provide a simple accompaniment to the hymns. In one of my present schools children who are about to take an examination perform their piece at an assembly and have found this very helpful to them for the examination. These children volunteer and no pressure is put upon them to perform. There are interesting assembly books to help teachers with suggestions for hymns and music, and also books on festivals and feasts from other cultures (see pages 110–114).

7 Assessment and recording

Assessment

The National Curriculum requires that assessment in music should be continuous, simple and flexible enough for teachers to be able to choose an approach which suits the needs of their pupils. There are no plans to produce national tests in music at key stages 1 and 2. Record keeping should be kept to a minium and should be sufficient to track curriculum progress and support the annual report to parents (Music non-statutory guidance E1).

With this in mind we need to ask ourselves first of all why are we assessing the children's musical education and ability? We can say that it will ensure that progression is shown, that there is a clear plan for the musical activities in any school and that it will not be the haphazard isolated experience that it has become in some cases. You will need to be aware of what previous musical experience the children have had in order to know what they have already achieved and what you are hoping they will achieve. You will have to decide who is going to do the assessment. It will involve the previous teachers, the visiting music specialist (if there is one) and the parents. If a mother tells you that her son practises his recorder every evening and is very keen to play for his relations at family gatherings or prefers to play to himself in his room or that her daughter sings her songs in the car or around the house or if you hear that a child shows an interest in the music on radio or remembers a song from a film or show, then all this needs to be taken into account. The children themselves need to be involved either in appraising their own performance or that of their peers, visiting musicians or recorded music. The reporting should be positive and related to aims and expectations. Assessment will therefore provide a benchmark against which individual pupils can be judged and can judge themselves over time. There will be a framework decided by the school for reporting to parents and continuity and progression can be shown over the key stages. This should help the teacher to plan future work.

Developing a framework

It is recommended that assessment should be continuous and in this framework we should gain an overall impression of an individual's progress using the attainment targets as aims. The development of the learning process should be emphasised. Rather than being a detached observer, the teacher should interact with the children and with the parents to enhance the children's musical experiences. You cannot assess all the children against the same criteria on the same task at the same time. You should watch out for a breakthrough in a child's understanding or a surprising or unusual reaction to the task in hand whether it is composing, or learning a song, or working with percussion or any of the varied and interesting musical opportunities provided both in and out of the classroom. You will also need to note evidence of any difficulty for example in holding a tune, in learning words or in producing musical ideas. Assessments are not made on purely teacher-initiated activities from a detached viewpoint. This means organising classrooms and the curriculum to provide space and time for some independent learning as well as structured teaching.

When assessing the child's musical capabilities you must not lose sight of the cross-curricular skills involved. You can note the child's co-ordination both in hand-eye dexterity when playing an instrument and reading a score, or at a simpler level playing whilst responding to a conductor's hand signals. Physical co-ordination is the most apparent skill whilst playing an instrument whether a recorder or a percussion instrument. You can notice whether a child appears to listen attentively with some understanding and shows awareness of subtle changes. Can the child express ideas, use the correct terminology and vocabulary? Is attention span being developed and is the child able to recall and imitate facts and ideas? Working together in groups, do the children show co-operation, perseverance, tolerance and concern for others? Is the child inventive, resourceful, expressive and responsive? What level of aesthetic appreciation does the child show? Is the child confident, self-motivated, self-disciplined and independent? All of these qualities may be apparent during the musical activities going on in the classroom and it is our job to record them.

Planning

Good planning is all important and it needs to be detailed and progressive. You need to discuss and agree with your colleagues what is the overall plan for music in the school and how you are going to achieve it. You need to agree what is targeted for assessment. Because there are to be no SATs for key stages 1 and 2 in music we can use this planning to keep records of children's progress. The teacher is therefore able to put emphasis on the positive achievements of the individual child so that no child needs to feel a failure where music is concerned. The accent should be on the positive and the opportunities given should cover such a wide range that every child achieves something. This does not mean that the expectations and opportunities for development and progression are low. There is a case for recording a particular achievement such as a solo spot during a performance, composition showing development of ideas, participation in extra curricular activities as well as comments from instrumental teachers and parents.

When making assessments we should be guided by the following principles:

1 Assessment should be part of the classroom process and be continuous.
2 Assessment should be taken from the widest practicable range of tasks and situations.
3 Extra curricular activities should be taken into account.
4 Attention should be paid to pupils' self assessment.
5 The process as well as the result should be assessed.
6 Pupils' achievements as part of a group should be assessed as well as individual performance.
7 All assessments made by everyone involved with the pupil should be taken into consideration including where appropriate, instrumental teachers.

Whether the teacher is assessing the child or group the following questions about classroom practice need to be asked:

1 Are there opportunities for
   listening?
   singing?
   composing?
   performing?
   working with music as 'sound'?
2 How often do these opportunities arise?
3 How is this organised? Do the children work as a class, in groups, in pairs or singly?
4 Are these experiences shared
   within the school?
   with other schools?

5 Do the children take decisions?
6 Does their music making contribute to the general level of education in the school?
7 Are the more specific needs of the child identified, for example, the musically gifted or physically handicapped?

If a control group is chosen then several sessions should be watched and assessment should not be made on the work of only one occasion.

You need to know the following:

1 Was the task completed?
2 Was the purpose of the task understood?
3 Were the pupils about to make decisions?
4 Did the resources extend the pupils' musical experiences through their own initiative?
5 Was the group extended in any other way?
6 Were their ideas expressed coherently, either musically or verbally?
7 Did their work have some shape (rhythmic, harmonic, medolic)?
8 Did all members of the group take part equally and work together harmoniously in a productive way?
9 Was there a leader?
10 Did the result demonstrate good use of the chosen instruments and have interesting sounds and dynamics?

You can assess the provision for music in your school for key stages 1 and 2 by asking the following:

1 What role is played by
   class teachers?
   the curriculum consultant?
   visiting specialists?
2 How is music made in the school?
   a Does the class teacher work with the visiting music specialist or the curriculum consultant and follow up any suggestions made by them?
   b Are all the staff involved in some form of music making?
   c Is there any other musical expertise in the school? This could include parents and friends, teachers with music as an outside interest.
   d Do you liaise with other schools, primary and secondary, to make or listen to music?
3 When is music made?
   a As it arises during the day?

   b Do all the classes make music?

   c Do you link music to other areas of the curriculum?

   d Do you make opportunities for team teaching thus sharing skills?

   e Is music making always timetabled?

   f How long do lessons last?

   g Are there opportunities for listening?

4 How do you use your resources?

   a Do you make full use of visiting specialists? Do you integrate their work with class music?

   b Are visiting artists in residence encouraged?

Peter McGowan, Royal Opera workshop leader with a pupil

   c Do you see time spent on out-of-school music activities as an extra or as an essential part of the children's musical education?

   d Are the instruments, music, CDs, cassettes and recording equipment easily accessible and kept in good repair?

   e Is recorded material available to the non-specialist?

   f Is there a scheme to give primary school children access to the more sophisticated equipment in secondary schools?

   g Are pupils taken to local concerts and recitals, amateur or professional, in order to demonstrate what can be achieved?

The non-statutory guidance to the National Curriculum for music sets out very clearly the criteria for assessment. Small children develop so quickly in the right environment that fairly detailed reports will need to be kept. You know immediately which children can sing in tune, or when given a percussion instrument or the chance to move to music immediately demonstrate a feeling and understanding of rhythm. You know which children when learning the recorder make music out of the row of notes learnt. You may now find children who cannot sing in tune but who have an interest in the history of music or in listening to tapes or who are able to compose a graphic score. In other words it will not be just the performers who are thought to be good at music. Simon (age 9) cannot sing in tune and has a poor sense of rhythm but he has a great interest in brass bands and collects tapes and talks knowledgeably about them. You need to know what music children are exposed to at home. Do they have experience of classical music or jazz or ethnic music? Have they an older relative who teaches them the songs from another era? Do either of their parents make music in any way? Andrew (age 6) had a great deal of help from his mother when he began to play the recorder. His mother found her recorder which she had not touched since her own schooldays and together they composed some simple three note tunes. There are some children who only listen to popular music, television or video, who have not had nursery rhymes or songs taught to them and this imbalance has to be redressed in school.

Recording achievement

Recording should be continuous and not based on one experience. The language used should be easily understood by the non-specialist. The purpose of recording is to inform the pupil and her/his parents where s/he is and what has been achieved. Each child should be treated as an individual and her/his opinions about the music being made and listened to should be considered alongside the observations being made by teachers, parents, visiting specialists or outside examining bodies if relevant.

The following charts are some ways of recording progress. The National Curriculum non-statutory guidance also contains suggestions for recording.

Name.................... Year....................

Record of musical activities

During this year I have experienced the following activities:

	often	sometimes
Singing in a group		
Singing solo		
Playing instruments solo		
Playing in a group		
Playing and singing together		
Listening to different types of music		
Playing and singing for an audience		
Singing solo for an audience		
Playing an instrument solo for an audience		
Composing in a group		
Composing alone		

How much did I enjoy each activity?

Pupil's name.................. Year...............

Music skills

Listening

Can the pupil ...	very easily	quite easily	with difficulty
1 recall a simple rhythm?			
2 recall a melody?			
3 follow simple notation?			
4 recognise changes of tempo and rhythm?			
5 identify instruments heard?			
6 identify changes in sounds?			
7 identify changes in mood?			
8 express verbally what the music means to them?			

Group composition

Does the pupil ...	consistently	often	sometimes
1 take the lead in shaping the composition?			
2 give ideas to the group?			
3 work well within the group, listening to the ideas of others?			

For the last twenty years I have been writing music profiles for children I have taught and the following are a few examples.

Neil (age 5)

Extrovert, friendly, very communicative.

Christmas

Has been in school for one term. Immediately showed great interest in drums, especially his 'favourite drum', the side drum. Has a very good rhythmic sense and can accompany any song or piece of music without direction. Can change rhythm very easily with the music. Likes to play rhythmic sequences. Can imitate a rhythm clapped to him without hesitation and can also improvise his own to fit in with the basic rhythm being sung or played. Shows great interest in music not only when in the music room but also with his class teacher who encourages his talent. He has produced with her a painted rhythmic pattern which he then played on the drum.

Easter

In spite of some bad health (rheumatic fever) which left him rather listless, he is still very interested. His parents have also shown interest and asked how they can encourage his talent. I advised them to buy him a drum and play as much good music of any kind as possible. He finds it difficult to play in a group situation but this should improve as he gets older. He enjoys recording his simple compositions in graphic notation but again prefers to work alone.

Summer

Neil has made friends with a girl and boy and will now play in a group situation with them. He will join in the class songs but his interest lies in instrumental music. He has recently asked for his 'tunes' to be written down in formal notation i.e. proper music, and has attempted to copy them.

Richard (age 6)

Introvert, very quiet, sensible, difficult to communicate with, slow to react.

Showed interest in musical instruments and has a good sense of rhythm. Shy at first but keen enough to play to overcome his shyness and volunteered to play the drum in the school concert.

Expresses very well his feelings towards music played for him. Said that slow music was 'deep and sad'. Recently became more communicative, and expressed his enthusiasm more freely. Recently he composed a three note tune but complained that he couldn't finish it, he was using **B C D** chime bars and asked for two lower notes. He picked out **G** and **A** chime bars and finished on **G**.

He has music at home, his father plays the guitar and they have a good selection of records. His parents are very pleased with his progress.

Danielle (age 10)

Introvert, timid, easily led. No musical background but has a good singing voice.

December
> Is beginning to play the recorder quite well. Able to read notes of treble clef. Some difficulty in recognising and reproducing rhythms. Sings well in tune but prefers to sing in a large group. Does not put forward many ideas when working in a group to create music. Listens intently to recorded music.

March
> Rhythmic work shows improvement as Danielle gains confidence. Still prefers to play and sing as part of a large group. Does not enjoy any form of performance, does not put forward any original ideas in group work. Enjoyed a visit with parents to a musical, wrote about her impressions of the show, very interested in the orchestra.

July
> Gaining in confidence. Recorder playing is very good, volunteered to play a short piece during a group composition. Still very nervous of solo performance. Enjoys listening to music and singing in the choir but refuses to sing solo, although quite capable of doing so. Parents report that she sings around the house but refuses to sing for anyone. Now an enthusiastic member of the school choir.

Mark (age 9)

Extrovert, cheerful, mischievous.

Thoroughly enjoys playing drums or tambourines. Has an excellent sense of rhythm and great style. Listens to a lot of popular music at home and is a good 'pop' dancer. Knows all the words of the current songs. Building on this, he enjoys any music with a strong sense of rhythm and is very interested in the instruments of the orchestra. He played in the band for the Christmas concert and showed a very good sense of timing. He remembered the sequence of items very well and had the appropriate instrument at the ready. He is interested in all forms of expression to music and painted 'making his brush dance' to the Polovtsian Dances (Borodin). He produced an extremely lively and colourful pattern. Recently he wrote a three note tune again with a strong rhythmic flavour. He is very keen to come into the music room whenever the opportunity arises. He has a very tuneful singing voice. He is not particularly academically inclined but he took great care and copied his tune our correctly.

He shows great interest also in the music in the classroom and uses many sound names in his stories. His class teacher is very interested in music and encourages his talent.

Mark is now showing interest in recording his musical work. He recently composed a rhythm on drum tins which inspired a machine for the drama work in his class.

Cheryl (age 8)

December

Cheryl sings well and learns songs very quickly. She enjoys adding an accompaniment to songs on small unpitched percussion instruments and has no difficulty maintaining a beat. She lacks confidence when asked to play pitched percussion instruments especially when a chord change is indicated. She has excellent sense of rhythm. She writes neat graphic notation scores in fine detail. She draws the instrument being played as well as the symbol. She is playing the descant recorder.

March

Cheryl can now hold a simple descant to songs with a group of other children. She obtains satisfaction from this singing in harmony. She is having piano lessons and is much more confident on glockenspiel and keyboard. She now wishes to compose using some formal notation. She is very precise and has to get everything just right. Prefers to play the keyboard. She is a keen member of the voluntary choir.

July

Cheryl is now composing simple tunes and writing them on the treble stave. She enjoys singing. She has a great interest in the recorder and has progressed beyond the class lessons in her book. She has written simple tunes for the recorder at the back of the tutor book. She enjoys listening to music but does not take part in class discussions as to what we have been listening to. She has very little music making at home. She spends a lot of time practising and her parents supply her with extra music books.

Due to the changes in curriculum it will now be necessary for every music specialist to work closely with class teachers and it will be a joint effort when the child is assessed against the end of key stage statements. In the past music could be a very isolated subject and the specialist could find that they taught children without having much knowledge of their ability or background. Now discussion should take place between teachers throughout the key stages. In order to make judgements about children, criteria must be established throughout the school under the guidance of the music specialist but with each teacher playing a part. The curriculum is now broad based and should offer every child an opportunity to shine. In no way should creative talent be destroyed because of insecure teaching. Teachers must know exactly what they are hoping to achieve and have a clear plan in mind in order to get there. The plan must be flexible and give room for the child to demonstrate any talent in any of the directions available. The stress should be positive. The ability to make and enjoy music is one of the great joys in life and should be presented as such.

8 General musical activities and resources

I Games

The following are games and activities that can be played at various times during the school day. They are played in a relaxed way but they reinforce many of the more formal activities in this book.

Sound Games

Vocal

1 On a given signal
   a sing a high sound to ah oh
   b sing a low sound
   c sing a quiet sound
   d sing a or b or c very quickly
   e sing a shape drawn in the air by the teacher or leader
   f sing a chant of people coming from a distance passing the school and going away again.
   eg We're going to put the *fire out*
       We're all *going* down to the *sand*
       We are the *best* in all this *land*

2 The teacher or leader can sing a sound. The children or child echoes it back as if they were a long way away.

3 The teacher sings a phrase to the children
   My name is Mrs Binns. Who are you?
   The children answer one at a time.
   My name is Johnny. How do you do?

4 Say and clap rhythmic chants.
   Who stole the cookies from the cookie jar?
   (Clap hands in time)

Johnnie did Johnnie did raa raa raa
(Clap hands together or with neighbour)

5 Clap and say name patterns.

James Brown Shilpi Sulha
This can be extended to include two or three names.

Jonathan Mary Lee

You can extend this by playing a singing game, 'Somebody's knocking at your door'. Choose two children with different name rhythms to hide behind a screen. One child claps her/his name rhythm after the word 'door' whilst the song is being sung. Donna whose name has been sung must decide whose name has been clapped. Increase the difficulty by increasing the number of children hiding. The game can be made more complex by the children singing the song moving round in a ring stopping when they sing 'door' to listen to the clapped rhythm. When Donna hears her name she goes into the middle to be ready to guess the name.

SOMEBODY'S KNOCKING

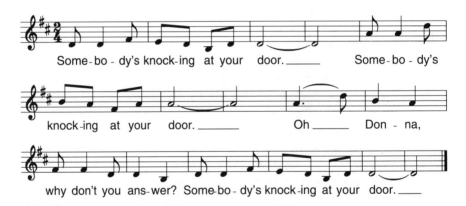

6 Play Chinese Whispers, the first child in a circle choosing a word or short phrase and whispering it to the next child in the circle, passing it on until the last child says it aloud and compares it with the first child's phrase. Then if it has changed check back to see where it changed.

7 Choose a word or phrase and say it in turn round the circle each child trying to say it in a different way eg loudly, quietly, slowly, quickly, in a high voice, in a low voice.

8 With older children give each child something to read, a book, a newspaper or magazine. Ask them to choose a short chapter. At a given signal all read together in response to a conductor, loudly, slowly, quietly, fast, loud getting quieter etc. Tape the result.

Instrumental

1 Hunt the instrument. Each child in the group has a sound-producing object. One child hides whilst an instrument already shown is hidden. As the child is hunting for the instrument the other children play loudly when 'hot' or near the hidden object, quietly when 'cold' or far away.

2 In a circle the teacher spins an instrument for example a drum or tambour and calls a child's name. If the child catches the instrument before it stops spinning s/he plays it.

3 Pass the instrument. An instrument is passed round a circle of children whilst a tape or another instrument is played by a child or the teacher. When the music stops the child holding the instrument plays it.

4 Each child in the circle has a sound-producing object. In turn the children make:
   a short sound
   a long sound
   a quiet sound
   a loud sound.
They must not play until the previous sound has died away.

5 Arrange your group into sets of instruments with sound either as above or:
   sounds on metal
   sounds on wood
   sounds on skin.
Using given signals conduct a pattern using the sets.

6 Using tambourines or drums or newspaper etc see how many different sounds can be made using the same material.

7 Hide a variety of different instruments or sound-producing objects in a box or behind a screen or cupboard. Ask the children to identify the object by its sound.

8 Make a 'surprise' sound on your instrument. Children stand in a circle with an instrument and in turn play their instrument in a 'different' or surprising way eg drums scratched, shakers tapped, cymbals stroked etc.

9 Listen to your heart beat. Play it on an instrument. Play it to accompany a well known song or nursery rhyme. Run around the room and then play your heartbeat. Notice the difference.

10 High and low. A child uses a pitched instrument, asks the class or group to close their eyes. Asks the group to stretch high when a high sound is played, low when a low note is played. When a glissando or slide is played everyone curls up into a ball.

Stretch high for a high note

11 A child takes one instrument or sound-producing object and a selection of beaters (two or three are usually sufficient) hides behind a screen and plays. The children guess which beater is used.

12 Children sit in a circle. Each child has an instrument (conventional or junk). The children join you playing whilst you lead with a drum. You change dynamic from loud to quiet, quiet to loud. Keep your rhythm constant, do not go faster and louder or slower as you get quieter.

Body Sounds

1 Build up a vocabulary of body sounds.

Head	knocking
	stroking
	tapping
Face	check popping
	teeth tapping
	scraping
	chattering
Chest	slapping
	rubbing
	thumping
	tapping
Hands	tapping
	clapping
	rubbing
	stroking
	knocking
	clicking
	strumming
	scraping
Knees	knocking
	tapping
Thigh	slapping
	stroking
Heel	stroking
	clicking
Feet	stamping
	tapping
	rubbing
	clapping soles together
	sliding

2 In a circle make a
     quiet body sound
     loud body sound
     short body sound
     long body sound
   in turn round the circle.

3 Play 'follow me'. One child makes a sound, the others copy it. This can be extended into a short sequence of sounds to copy.

4 Cumulative game in a small group in which one makes a sound, the next makes that sound and adds one of her/his own and so on.

5 First child says 'I have a present for you' and makes a sound. The next child says 'Thank you for the ***' and repeats the sound. The second child then turns to the third child and says 'I have a present for you' and makes her/his own sound. The third child says 'Thank you for the ***' and repeats the sound given, then turns to the fourth child and so on around the circle.

6 Make flashcards of words of sound for example clicking, hitting, rubbing, blowing. Ask the child to make the sound described on the card.

7 Decide on a signal for Simon Says. It could be on chime bars
     C C E.
   Give the children instructions that only when **C C E** are played on chime bars or glockenspiel should they follow your instruction to, for example, touch their head etc (children will need to have played Simon Says to understand this game).

8 Tap out the rhythm of the first line of a well known song or nursery rhyme. Ask the children to identify it by its rhythm. The child who answers correctly taps out her/his choice of song.

9 Ask the children to sit in a circle. First child claps once, and then the next, and so on in a clockwise direction. The clap is passed on in a steady rhythm until the teacher or first child calls out 'change' and then the clap is passed back in an anti-clockwise direction until change is called again. Then try to do the same with eyes shut.

10 When listening to a rhythmic piece of music on tape perhaps being played whilst the children are coming into or going out of assembly, the teacher or leader can perform a rhythmic pattern perhaps tapping head, shoulders, knees and then clapping hands. The children imitate the movements and watch carefully to see if the movements change. The pattern becomes more complicated with practice. These patterns are often closely allied with hand jiving when done with other children.

Traditional singing games

Singing games have been a favourite activity in playgrounds all over the world. Children carry out the most complicated skipping, clapping and chanting patterns often much more difficult than we would expect them to do in class. I taped a series of children's singing games and was surprised by their complexity. Some traditional games are:

> *Ring-a-ring o' roses*
> *There was a princess long ago*
> *The big ship sails on the ally ally oh*
> *The farmer's in his den*
> *In and out the dusty bluebells.*

All these ring games and singing chants have instant appeal. The words and rhythms are simple, repetitive and therefore easily learnt. The actions combine with the singing and encourage the children to sing out freely. Many of the games have an historical context such as Ring-a-ring o' roses which is about the great plague of London. The posies are the herbs being carried to ward off the disease, and the 'all fall down' is self explanatory! Investigation into the history of games and nursery rhymes is a project worth undertaking by older children. There is also now a wealth of games from other countries being played in our playgrounds.

II Listening and appraising recorded music

An extensive repertoire of attractive, stimulating music needs to be chosen to stimulate the children. You cannot expect them all to enjoy everything played to them but you can give them something to listen to, and discuss why they like or dislike what they hear. You need to respect their opinions and to listen to, and give an opinion on their own choice of music. Above all you need to encourage them to listen. You can do this by not playing the music for too long a period at a time, and by exposing them to as many different types of music as possible from many countries and cultures. You can play European classics, from early to modern, jazz, regional music from the British Isles and music from as many cultures as you can find. You must make the listening interesting by pointing out the use of different types of instruments, of rhythms, and with older children, of simple structure. You can relate the music to the social history of the time, for example Victorian music hall songs, sea shanties, work and protest songs. You can tell the story of any programme music or opera or ballet you listen to. You can discuss with the children what emotions the music evokes in them.

LIBRARY, UNIVERSITY COLLEGE CHESTER

III Resources

Book title	Author/Compiler	Publisher
General books		
Make Music	Collini/Goretti	Arnold Wheaton
My Class Makes Music	V. Lee	Franklyn Watts
Our Steel Band	R. Warner	Wayland
Sing a Song, Bks 1 and 2	W. Bird, G. McAulisse	Nelson
Sound Waves	L. Davies	Collins
Music	M. Hart	Heinemann
Sound Ideas	P. Binns, M. Chacksfield	OUP
Oxford Primary Music	J. Gilbert L. Davies	OUP
Song books		
Apussikidu	Harrop, Blakeley, Gadsby	A & C Black
Okki Tokki Unga	Harrop, Friend, Gadsby	A & C Black
High Low, Dolly Pepper	V. Clark	A & C Black
Mango Spice	Cameron, Connolly, Singham	A & C Black
Tinder Box	Barratt, Hodge	
Music from the Past	A. and M. Bagenal	Longman

Book title	Author/Compiler	Publisher

Books with a musical theme

Book title	Author/Compiler	Publisher
Madam Nightingale will Sing Tonight	J. Mayhew	Orchard
Sleeping Nana	K. Crossley	Orchard
Bertie and the Bear	P. Allen	Hamish Hamilton
There's a Hole in my Bucket	W. Stobbs	OUP
Fox went out on a Chilly Night	P. Spier	Picture Puffin
The Happy Hedgehog Band	J. Barton, M. Waddell	Walker

Reference books

Book title	Author/Compiler	Publisher
Sound and Silence	J. Paynter, P. Aston	CUP
New Sounds in Class	G. Self	Universal
Children Using Language	A. Jones, J. Mulford	OUP
Modern Educational Dance	R. Laban	Macdonald & Evans
Pop, Rock and Ethnic Music	G. Vulliamy E. Lee	OUP

Wall charts, packs and visuals

Instruments	4 poster pack of some of the instruments of the orchestra.
Indian Musical Instruments Indian Dance	Pack of 8 charts looking at Indian music.
What is music?	Chart showing concepts of pitch, duration, timbre, dynamics and tempo.

All available from:
Pictorial Charts Educational Trust
27 Kirchen Road
London
W13 0UD

Flannelgraph

Treble and bass staff and clefs with notes, accidentals, etc to stick on and take off when required.

Available from:
Resource
Exeter Road
Coventry Road
Doncaster
DN2 4PY

The telephone and how it works

Available from:
British Telecom
Education Service
PO Box 10
Wetherby
Yorkshire
LS23 7E

Light and sound primary science pack

Available from:
Molehill Press
Grange Farmhouse
Feddington
Kettering
Northamptonshire
WN14 1AL

Computer software

Sound ideas
Touching sound
Ensemble

Available from:
NCET Publications
Sir William Lyons Road
Science Park
Coventry
CV4 7EZ

Sound worlds

Available from:
Hybrid Technology Ltd
273 The Science Park
Cambridge
CB4 4WE

Some useful addresses

Aklowa Cultural Centres
Takeley House
Brewers End
Takeley
Nr Bishops Stortford
Herts
(*Workshops, mainly West African.*)

The Amateur Music Association
Medlock School
Wadesan Road
Manchester 13
(*Advisory and information services open to individuals and groups.*)

Indian Music Promotions
The Manor House
The Green
Southall
Middlesex
(*Supply Indian music cassettes. folk instruments, dances costumes and books.*)

Tapes and compact discs

The following is a list of recorded music mainly classical that we have found useful, but popular music folk and jazz must not be forgotten.

Hungarian Dances Brahms
Air from Suite No. 3 Bach
Magnificat Bach
Brandenburg Concertos Bach
The Emperor Concerto (5th) Beethoven
Egmont Overture Beethoven
Piano Sonata (Moonlight) Beethoven
Piano Sonata (Pastoral) Beethoven
The Nutcracker Suite Tchaikovsky
Capriccio Italien Tchaikovsky
Music for Romeo and Juliet Tchaikovsky
Swan Lake Ballet Music Tchaikovsky
1812 Overture Tchaikovsky
Music for a Midsummer Night's Dream Mendelssohn
Comedians' Gallop Kabalevsky
Magic Fire Music, The Valkyries Wagner
Russian Sailors' Dance Glier
The Pines of Rome Respighi
Festivals Debussy
Clair de Lune Debussy

L'Après Midi d'un Faune Debussy
Carnival of the Animals Saint-Saëns
Danse Macabre Saint-Saëns
Peter and the Wolf Prokofiev
Pictures at an Exhibition Musorgsky
Overture to the Magic Flute Mozart
La Boutique Fantasque Rossini
Piano Concertos and Studies Chopin
The Rite of Spring Stravinsky
Valse Triste Schubert
Sea Symphony Vaughan Williams
Noyes Fludde Britten
Midsummer Night's Dream Britten
Gymnopédies 1 and 2 Satie
Rhapsody in Blue Gershwin
Surprise Symphony Haydn
Toy Symphony Haydn
Karelia Suite Sibelius
Valse Triste Sibelius
Finlandia Sibelius
Till Eulenspiegel's Merry Pranks Richard Strauss
Rodeo — Appalachian Spring Aaron Copland
Symphony No. 2 — The Lark Ascending Vaughan Williams
The Planets Suite Holst

It is impossible to list all the music that could be of use in school but these are some that could provide the starting point of a collection. If the music of one composer provokes interest it can become the basis of a musical exploration.

We also listen to the music of the Beatles, some of whose songs are now found in collections of children's songs, Bob Dylan, Eric Clapton and traditional and modern jazz. We can also be on the 'listen' for any popular music that may suit our purpose eg providing a song for a theme or topic.

Conclusion

This book has described some of the ways that children can become aware of sounds in their environment, how to organise patterns of sound in order to become aware of the difference between various sounds, and through these activities to be introduced to the elements in music. The activities described are well within the capabilities of most teachers. They do not need to be 'musical' to introduce musical activities to young children. They can with enthusiasm and sensitivity, obtain results which are exciting and worthwhile. All the musical activities described in this book can be used in the classroom and it has been found that within a carefully planned framework the children will lead the teacher forward. I do not believe that music teaching in the primary school should be the sole responsibility of one music specialist but that every class teacher can teach music and let it supplement all the other creative work in the curriculum. If there is a music specialist on the staff then it is very useful to have help with the more formal aspects of music, but the absence of such a teacher should not inhibit us or deprive children of the joy of singing, composing and listening to music. I have over the past 22 years met children who say that they cannot sing but I have yet to meet a child who says that s/he is unable to listen to music or to play a simple percussion instrument. Children enjoy making and listening to music. It takes a great deal to spoil the subject.

Music can become an important part of school life. Children eventually see it in its place just as they see science or reading. Many children, unable to shine in other disciplines, find in music an opportunity to achieve. Alan (age 7) was disruptive and always in trouble but in the recorder class he was the best. Jenny (age 9) had just arrived from another school and was trying to find her place within the class. She soon became the girl with the good voice. I have tried to show that music can be a source of inspiration for art, language, drama and dance. In no other discipline have the abilities of young children been so underrated.

Young children have the ability to take in the essentials of music in a clear and uncomplicated way. They grasp the essentials unclouded by inhibitions or pre-conceived ideas of form. They create real music full of life and innovations. We can use this enthusiasm and creativity as a foundation on which to teach the more formal aspects of music. I am not advocating 'scribble periods' or 'free expression' but a carefully planned progression and extension using the young child's curiosity about the world of music and sounds. If we are successful then we can provide our children with a lifelong interest which will help them to fill their leisure time, satisfy their emotions, give them a great deal of pleasure and enable them to give pleasure to others. Many teachers are afraid of tackling music, but now the National Curriculum makes it a requirement for primary schools to teach music. Teach it with joy and enthusiasm using your own strengths on which to build and, speaking from experience, you will find the task very satisfying and exciting — you will be amazed at where the children will take you.

Index

acoustics 72–80
African drums 82
amplification 79
appraisal 54, 64, 65–66, 109–110
assemblies 2, 90
assessment 91–102
audiometers 80

background noise 26
beat 66–67
  see also rhythm
Bird, Wendy, *Sing a Song* 17
body sounds 107–109
brass instruments 75
breath 8, 9, 78

cadence 61
carols 17–18, 67, 69
chants 53–54, 70–71
Chinese number song 5
choreography 85
classroom practice 93–94
classrooms
  classroom sounds 25, 27–29
  music areas 49–50
  sound corners 21
composition 52–55, 61–71, 82
  songs 16–19, 64–66, 67–69
  sound patterns 26–27
  sound stories 41–44, 54
  soundscapes 15–16
confidence 7–8
creative writing 44–47
  see also poems, stories
criticism *see* appraisal
cross-curricular links 81–90
  see also science and sound

dance 83–86
diction 8, 9
duration 37, 76–77
dynamics 36–37

Egyptian notation 86–88
environmental sounds 23–25,
    48–49, 54–55
  noise 26, 41–42, 79

frequency 74

games 103–109
graphic notation 27–29, 30–31,
    56–59, 62, 86–88
group assessment 94

harmony 14, 15
history 86
Holst, *The Planets* 82–83
home environment 91, 96
  sounds and noises 26, 48–49
Hughes, Ted, *The Iron Man* 52–53
humming 9
hymns 90

instruments
  children's descriptions 48
  choice and effect 82
  'doctoring' 38, 64, 66
  games 105–107
  how they work 75–78
  music areas 49–50
  see also percussion,
    unconventional instruments

junk instruments *see*
    unconventional instruments

kettle chant 53

language
  and music 39–55
  of sound 26
  sung language 10
  see also terminology; vocabulary
listening 72–73, 89, 109–110
  listening walks 43

machine sounds 10, 11
measuring sound 79, 80
movement 11
Mozart, *Eine kleine
    Nachtmusik* 44–47
music rooms 1
Musorgsky, *Night on a Bare
    Mountain* 85

name patterns 33
National Curriculum 91
noise 26, 41–42, 79
notation 51–52
  Egyptian 86–88
  graphic 27–29, 30–31, 56–59, 62
  staff (conventional) 56, 60–61

ostinato 70–71
Owl Song 65

painting 44–45, 82–83
parents
  and assessment 91, 96
  in school 3, 77
part singing 14
pentatonic scales 66
percussion 20–38
  scoring 56–59, 60–61
  and vibration 76
performing 14, 90
pianos, 'doctored' 38
pitch
  awareness 7–8, 34–35
  improving 9
  and vibration 73–74
planning 92–93
poems
  by children 41, 54–55, 82, 85–86
  ostinato 70–71
  as stimulus for composition 52
programme music 61
pulse *see* rhythm

rainforest soundscape 15–16
recorded music 109–110
  suggestions 44, 61, 82, 113–114
records of progress 96–102
resources 110–114
  instruments 20, 21
rhythm 32–34, 66–67
  see also ostinato
rounds 14

Saint-Saëns, *Carnival of the Animals* 40
schools, music provision 94–96
science and sound 72–80
scoring 30–31, 56–71
Sibelius, *Finlandia* 82
singing 5–11, 14–16
  games 104, 109
  see also songs
snare drum, child's description 48
solfa 14, 60–61

songs
  choice 6, 12, 13–14
  composition 16–19, 64–66, 67–69
  teaching 12–14
sound
  language of sound 26
  and science 72–80
sound frames 22–23
sound patterns 26–27
sound poems 54–55
sound stories 41–44, 54
sound waves 72, 77
sounds
  classroom 25, 27–29
  environmental 23–25, 48–49, 54–55
  see also noise
soundscapes 15–16
staff (conventional) notation 60–61
  drawbacks 56
stories
  songs for stories 16–17
  sound stories 41–44, 54
Stravinsky, *Firebird* 85
string instruments 75–76
sung language 10

tables calypso 13
tambourines 29–30, 30–31, 37
Tchaikovsky, *Waltz in D* 84
teaching aids 49–50
terminology 26, 39–40, 66
themes 81
  light and dark 85
  power 82–83
  winter 61–63
timbre 75
tone-deafness 9

unconventional instruments 21, 22, 52–53
  pitch investigation 73–74

vibration 72–78
vocabulary 40–41, 50–52, 107
  see also terminology
voice 5–19
  how it works 78–79
  vocal games 103–105

washing machine music 11
wind instruments 75
workcards 33, 49–50
world music 88–89
writing about music 44–47, 48, 50–51, 55, 63